...from Spirit to Spirit...

a real life story of a woman

a guide to overcome the conditioning of social and environmental hypnosis

by:
Rev. L. Manonne Fontainne, O.M.,C.Ht.

Lizbette Manonne Fontainne, O. M., C. Ht.

...from Spirit to Spirit...

a real life story of a woman

a guide to overcome the conditioning of social and environmental hypnosis

by:
Rev. L. Manonne Fontainne, O. M., C.Ht.

Published by T.H. F.T.C. Publishing, a division of The Healing Feeling Transformation Center

Contents

Acknowledgments

First and without hesitation I am grateful to God, for giving life and love not only to me, but to everything around me. Further I cannot detail all other gifts for which I am grateful to God, since my conscious mind is still too limited to comprehend the magnitude and abundance of His limitless generosity.

I am grateful to every being who volunteered to take part in the shaping and growing of this writer's development. Thank you for all your contributions to my life.

On a singular count my deepest appreciation must be delivered to the spirit of my ever living grandmother - Terezia - for being my first Angel.

To Carla - for dusting off the path of my soul, so I could shine the light of my own spirit in the direction I know I must head and - without hesitation - follow. My second Angel.

To Kathy - (a fictitious name) for opening the door to the basement of my mind and letting out the monsters. My third Angel.

To Dr. Deepak Chopra - for merging modern science and ancient theology - physical and spiritual realities into a brand new, harmoniously resonating consciousness - for the entire human race, for me - to embrace without conscious effort. My fourth Angel.

To my children: Robert and Kelly - (a fictitious name) for choosing me to bring forth God's gift of life in them. Thank you, my forever Angels.

To my husband, John - for being my twin flame. For showering me with love, tenderness, patience, encouragement and understanding, yet not flooding out the cause. Thank you for your faith, my twin Angel.

To my editor, Phillys Bergman - for her patience and knowledge, for taking a manuscript and turning it into a piece of wonderful work without changing its direction and personality. Thank you, wise Angel.

To my many, many healed and healing clients - for their courage and daring to go forward to try something new. For their own love and faith in God and in their own selves. Thank you rising Angels.

To Lori Bateman, my technical advisor - for the many suggestions and physical contributions. Thank you, all.

The Little Things

Don't ever outgrow the little things, that God just gives
away,
The free fresh air and sunshine and the games that
robins
play.

Don't ever outgrow the magic of a puddle in the
rain,
The splash a little pebble makes, the joy a rainbow
contains.

Don't ever outgrow big shady trees with shadows twice
their size,
Or the magic of the perfect moon that captivates your
eyes.

Don't ever outgrow the tender heart that loves the
things it sees,
And clings to all that's beautiful in treasured memories.

(Reverend) Manonne and her husband John live and work in Cedar Rapids, Iowa. She is founder and director of the Healing Feeling Transformation Center® for life style modification as well as the Spirits of the Golden Light - a Spiritual Assembly for the purification and upliftment of the human soul, which she minister.

A Certified Hypnotherapist, Ordained Minister and Certified Spiritual Healer, she specializes in all forms of chemical dependencies, addictive behaviors, management of depression and stress, fear and anxiety, self esteem and self improvement. She is a counselor of spiritual elevation and healing.

She is a frequent speaker and lecturer on chemical dependencies, domestic violence, child abuse and self abuse as well as general dysfunction. She speaks with total honesty and from personal experience.

She welcomes your comments, opinions and interests on all of the subjects discussed in this book.

In addition to private practice and public speaking, she presently is working on her second book: *Genesis: 3-5. A dialogue with Eve.*

She can easily be contacted through:

The Healing Feeling Transformation Center®
PO Box 8583 Cedar Rapids, IA 52408-8583

Forewords

Some people say: "You have to be famous before you write a book about yourself."

Yet others, like my husband say: "You have so much to share! God, I can't get enough of your words!"

The story that you are about to read is mine and mine alone. It is my *perception* of myself and my experiences. Some names of people and places have been changed deliberately to avoid causing discomfort to anyone who affected my life and is still alive today.

The *wisdom* in my words is not mine. They come to me from God in various forms of messages, for God gives me his understanding.

You may or may not believe any of these writings. That is a *choice* we all have. My reason for writing this story? At the end, it will all be clear.

This book is based on *forty two* years of pain, struggle, confusion, deceit, abuse and self abuse; three years of *searching* and *finding* and finally achieving a life of pure joy, happiness and bliss, power- full enough to erase all negative emotions of my past.

If you are looking for a gentle book for fireside reading, this one is not for you. If you are able to follow through the thorny road of a life and accept the raw truth of each word, yet have no pity or sadness; if you have a need to believe that people can and do change and *transform* into balanced human beings, and utilize each of their experiences as a tool in nurturing others still very much in pain, so they too can unleash and free that beautiful self called *spirit,* and create a lifelong contract with their *ego,* so together they can live in natural harmony in this earthly temple we call body; then I embrace you with *unconditional love* strong enough to provide you with all the energy you will need to finish reading each word. Have no judgment, anger or disappointment. I have none. Rather, I wish for you the feelings of joy and peace that I now feel and forever will, which I have found through forgiveness, acceptance, surrender and serenity, living in God's Grace.

I Love You - One and All.

Part I

Chapter 1

Blinking at Consciousness

The morning of May 17, 1989 was no different to me from any other morning. In fact, it could have been any morning in May, September or January for that matter. It could have been any morning in any God given year. It did not matter. Nothing much mattered anymore. Most of the time I didn't care if it was morning, day or night. Most of the time I did not know. What did matter was, that I was alone with my chemical gods: Mr. Coke and Mr. Gallo. A few ounces of the first, a few gallons of the second. They were all I needed and wanted. My silent gods. Everyone else was my enemy. I loved my silent gods. We took each other seriously. *We took each other!* We kept each other faithful company. I was loyal to them and they kept me *free*. Free of *feelings*, free of *sensations,* free of *emotions*. I took them everywhere with me. From one room of my house into the other: first floor, second floor, into the garden. Everywhere. We were *committed!* We had loyalty! On this particular morning we went camping together. I crawled under my dining room table, with my gods protecting me. One in my pocket one in my lap. The table cover hung over the edges of the table, creating the illusion of a tent. Yeah, we were camping, we were happy, the three of us! Together. Both my husband and daughter had gone to work long before I crawled out of bed. I usually planned it that way. I would wake up about 3 or 4 AM and gulp a quart or so of Gallo, before returning to bed. Insurance. To make sure I could not be awakened in the morning, while the two of them got ready for their day.

It was so peaceful camping there all by myself! I didn't even hear the door open and someone enter the house. I didn't know who it was looking into my tent, even after I saw his face peering into mine. He seemed to have known me though, because he crawled right into my tent and sat down directly in front of me. I thought: 'I gotta get a larger place, this one is way too small to have company in!' I had the *sensation* of him taking my hand in his . Then, he took my chin and lifted up my head. I do not know if he wanted to see my face or for me to see his. I couldn't focus my eyes, nor could I collect enough strength to hold my own head up. So, he cupped my face in both his palms and kept looking at me for what may have been eternity.

As he began to speak I was wishing he would disappear! 'An uninvited stranger messing with my peace and crowding my spacious tent! Now, the bastard was noisy, too!' I had no energy to make a sound and he couldn't care less about my *desire* for privacy. He just kept on talking and talking. I gave in and he kept on. Something about a bird. He was talking about a bird.

'I like birds,' I thought, and slowly his words created a *focus*.. His voice was gentle and soothing, if somewhat shaky here and there. I listened.

"It was a very large bird," he said, "bigger than any other bird in his neighborhood. At one time he was a great bird! Strong, powerful, independent. But not no more! Today, he was sitting alone at the slimy edge of the marshes in the green, dirty mirk of filth. No self-respecting bird would go near him. He had been sitting there in that cold, forboding spot for a long, long time. No food to eat, no fresh water to drink. His feathers had been covered with mud, dried on, hard and solid. Even the clouds cast constant shadows over him, as to intensify his misery and self pity. He kept thinking about his past. Once-upon-a-time-long-ago, when his life was filled with family and friends and flights far above the clouds, where the sky was blue, the air was pure and the sun shone and glistened on his beautiful feathers. A time long, long ago. As the bird sat there, dreaming of his past, he had a strong *desire* to be that bird

12

again. 'What had gone wrong?' he wondered. It didn't matter. He kept on *dreaming, wishing, visualizing.* Suddenly, the clouds broke and a small ray of sunshine beamed down, directly onto the bird. Then a thicker ray, an entire shaft of sunlight! He noticed but did not move. That beautiful sunray kept right on beaming down, warming the bird and slowly he moved one of his wings - just a little. A clump of mud fell away from his wing and the bird sensed a sudden *lightness*, as if some of his sorrow broke free. And the sun kept sending that wonderfully warm ray down on him. The clouds opened wider, filled with the golden ray and more and more mud dried, than fell off of the bird. He rose himself a tad, then gently shook, to shed even more of his burden, as the golden ray, with its warmth, deeply penetrated beyond his feathers and his body began to come alive. There was magic between that golden sunlight and the bird! Soon, he felt strong enough to stand and spread both his wings. He spread them high and wide and shook his entire body, his head, his tail, casting aside the mud, breaking free of his *prison.* 'What a miracle!' the bird thought. 'If I could, just once more fly!' And a voice from some *unknown source* answered: "You could, if you would only try!" Hearing that voice, the bird took a deep breath, positioned himself for lift-off and pushed upward.   He spread his wings and flapped with all his might and pushed himself up to another majestic flight, never looking back."

I listened with awe and great attention. Then, my speaker stayed quiet for a second. As he fell silent I heard my own voice muse:

"Wow! That's cool!" I looked into his eyes and recognized him. He was the person who supplied my drugs. My own dealer! He said one more thing:

"Manonne, that bird was a phoenix. You are that phoenix. Have a dream and go out there - go for it!"

"I already have a dream," I said and lifted up the end of the table cover. It was no longer my tent wall. There was a beam of sunlight which poured in through the window directly under the dining table, onto the spot where was I sitting .   At that moment something happened to me. *Something I could not explain then and I no longer try.* I crawled out from under the table, taking with me my stash and wine. When I stood up, I was completely sober. *For the first time in forty two years, I had no head-ache, no nausea, no dizziness and I stood steady!* Hm. I found myself smiling as I headed toward the bathroom.

I flushed the drugs I had in my hand down the toilet, then collected and flushed all the back-up, as well.
I figured, about two thousand dollars went down the drain.

May 17, 1989 was the last day of my drug use and addiction. I did not know much about phoenixes in those days, but that story was good enough to make an impression on me. I did not give up my wine though, not for a few more years to come. It took more than a dirty bird to part with that. When I did, it was in May, also. Something about May and Me.

I have never been arrested for drug possession, use, or for any other reason. I have never provided another living being with drugs. I was way too selfish for that! Alcohol, yes. In fact, upon reading this book will be the first time my family and friends will become aware of my drug addiction. At least to my knowledge. I kept it in a closet.

I learned much in those eight years, between '81 and '89, though often I did not remember. As I used, I sometimes asked myself the same question most other addicts do: "Why?" I had no answer. I just used.

Today, when I am in the company of a person who is strung out, I don't see a useless addict or messed up junky. I see a person in deep, deep pain, pain that has no name, no beginning and *seemingly* no end. A pain that I now understand better than they do. Deep in my spirit I know and believe that their pain too can heal and stay where it belongs - in the past - as does mine.

As I hold my arms open to embrace whoever is in front of me, I seldom see a body. I hold close to me a wounded spirit and confused soul, filled with the lies of their own ego and the truths of *other people*. It does not matter to me if he or she is dirty, drunk or beyond reasoning. I reach into the depths of their spirit and love it without question, reason or *expectations.*

It is up to them to take that love or block it out. No one can make a difference to a person if they are not *receptive.* Still, to take that first step, to reach out, is my *destiny* in life, and my *destination.* For getting ill or getting well is an act of the *free will.* You have to *volunteer* to give, also to receive. Life is so simple! Give and take. Breathe in, breathe out. That is all.

That morning by far had not been my day to get well. Instead, it became the first day of many weeks and even months of pain, confusion, fear, guilt and finally *letting go* of what was and *receiving life* and *love* itself.

I hid Mr. Gallo god in his usual place. It did not even occur to me to part with it. My storyteller left, leaving behind him another bird awaiting some bumpy flights. Not a great phoenix, but a battered little bird of a sparrow. It was the last time I saw my dealer. My addiction was a secret. I kept it in the closet - more than one way. I have never missed the drugs, just as I don't miss the alcohol or cigarettes or food, for that matter.

My drug days began in 1981 during the time I lived in the South Pacific. I was the Islands' *sweetheart* and *princess* and my desires were the natives' wish to fulfill. We got along well. When the time came to return to the *real world,* I was sad to leave.

There was a changed person inside my body. Not good, not bad, only different. Something was different. I felt a kind of loss, rather than a gain. An echo. I had no emotions of sadness or fear. Those came later. Perhaps a sense of emptiness, as if some part of me took flight and left with that bird. I did not know. For that *moment* all was O.K. For that moment. For that *present moment.*

The moment, however, passed and future moments came into place and each following moment hit me like a wave of an angry ocean. By the mid hours of the afternoon I was fast losing *control.* The waves of my emotions pounded on me so fierce and fast, I had no chance to name them! My body trembled and I fell onto my knees. *Fear* and *panic* took possession of my entire being.

With all the strength I could gather, I crawled into my bedroom. My heart raced and I was choking on my own *anxiety.* All I wanted was to get into bed and die! Oh, forget the bed, just die! 'Dear God, please let me be a total coward and let me die!' I pleaded. Someone inside my head roared in a hideous laughter: "What God? You flushed me down the toilet!" I propped myself up against the side of my bed and began to cry. My body was soaking in its own sweat. I had no idea if the salt on my lips came from my tears or my sweat.

I kept on crying, crying, crying! A voice echoed as if coming from an immeasurable distance. It was my own voice saying: "You are not the God I want! I want the real God! *The real God.* Please, oh please, help me!"

Then, it happened. Somehow, in an instant I was way up in the corner of the ceiling, looking down onto what I knew was my body. I was overcome by a kind of compassion totally new to me. Down there was my flesh, propped up like some lifeless doll, shaking with wave after wave of convulsive cries, filled with agony and desperation, pain and hopelessness. I looked down on my self with a deep and *pure love*, only God could have sent. The real God. Without a sound or even a thought, I sent myself a feeling:

"I love you. We'll be O.K. I love you."

And with that, back I was in that broken little body. I stopped crying, lay flat onto the carpet and fell asleep.

16

Time had no meaning. I have no idea how much time that *drama* of my life occupied. When I awoke I was still alone, at home and safe. The sun was leaving the day, but left in my memory a horizon painted more beautiful than any other day's end. I was painting also, in those days and had recalled the colors of that evening from my memory, often.

It was a gift from God, I knew. From the *real God!* With it he painted my *spirit*.

As I stood at the window of my studio inhaling those last rays, a thought came to me: 'I am going back to New York in the morning. Just me. Without saying a word to anyone. Discussion would be meaningless. I will simply write two letters: one to my husband and one to my daughter. I'll be gone for two weeks, maybe three.'

The sun was over the horizon.

Life goes on.

July, 1948, with my parents.

Chapter 2

Onward, Little Soldier

Though I woke up early the following morning, I remained in bed, pretending to be asleep. Eager to get on my way, yet not too eager to cause any suspicion. No need to divert from our comfortable and accepted routine of middle class life. The door barely shut behind my husband and daughter, I was out of bed.

Into the shower, out of the shower! Hair blown fluffy, thanks to Vidal Sasson!

Coffee in one hand, mascara in the other my mind racing, scanning through the contents of my closet. 'What to pack? Where is the suitcase? Do I even have one? Who cares!'

'Remember to make the bed. Be sure to have the house 'House Beautiful' camera ready! Don't forget to write the two letters!' I said out loud. Twenty minutes passed, I was ready: battered body, shaken soul, hopeful spirit, old suitcase, new attitude! Well, at least my clothes were their usual selves.

9:30 AM, May 18, 1989. 'There is a world out there and a place in it for me. I'll find it!'

Aspirin, credit cards.   'I'll need to gas up the Thunderbird. Map, address book, notebook and pen. I don't have a Bible! It's O.K. Hotels do. Don't forget Tom Bodette and his Motel 6 list. Traveling first class.' I laughed out loud:

"Well, at least Tom will leave the light on for me." 'Take your sense of humor, too!' I was already in an unusually good mood.

10:00 AM. House locked. Car is packed. I am sitting at the steering wheel of the car, having a meaningful conversation with myself: 'I am ready!'

'Sure?'

'Yeah!'

    'Where in the hell do you think you are going?'
    'East, I am going to New York.'

    "Dear God, the real one, I am not very good at this, but if you have a little spare time, would you keep an eye on me? Only one eye's enough. I know you are busy and really, only if you have some spare time. Just in case I get scared or something. You know what I mean. Thanks."

    I drove into the morning, heading toward Montana. It was a beautiful, warm day already. The sun rose at the peak of the tallest mountain with a display of colors as rich as the one he left behind in my memory the night before.
I was filled with *expectancy* and apprehension. At Drummond, Montana, the weather changed. All of a sudden I was driving in the middle of a winter blizzard! The snow fell as balls, instead of flakes! I had to pull off the highway and park at the edge of it. I was on the edge! As if on cue, my fear of whatever overpowered me and I broke into a cry. Again and again emotions pounded on my heart and soul. I tasted the salt of my tears as I wiped my tongue over my lips. I kept on weeping, just like yesterday.
    "Dear God, is it to soon to ask? Will this ever end? Will I ever be able to at least name these waves of torment! Will I ever have a day, just one day, when I feel good? Five minutes? One? What am I running from or to? What am I doing, anyway?" I had no answers, only my internal fears. I was overwhelmed by fear of the unknown, by the lack of natural experiences in my life. I thought of turning around and going back home. But I didn't have a home! Only a building with lots of stuff in it and some empty spaces here and there. Empty spaces. I was afraid of ever going back to those empty spaces. I was afraid of everything, so I just kept on sitting in my car, there, at the edge of the road, waiting for something to happen. As the storm passed outside, it slowly passed inside of me as well.

'It never rains in Southern California... maybe I should move back there... hell, no, I cried there, too!...All emotions pass...All emotions pass...' My thoughts both tempted and entertained me.

I heard trucks pass by me. Time to get going. Montana is a beautiful state any time of the year, even if you are unaware of being in it.

Casper, Wyoming. It's dark. Best to find the light Tom left on for me. Some food, too.

My first night alone, totally alone since July 1965. Hm. The truth is, I have been alone all of my life!

The phone call to home was not received with tremendous joy. Understandable.

"I will be home on June 11th..." Silence.

"Whatever I am doing...well I really am not sure. I only know that I had to get out or I will die. I just had to..." Silence.

"I don't know what will happen when I get back. I do know that life for me will not be the same. It can't be. Not ever. I also know that I'm willing to take responsibility for whatever changes will come..." Silence.

"If I were drunk right now, I would probably keep carrying on a one-way conversation, but I am not drunk, so I feel pretty stupid talking to a smelly, black piece of plastic all alone in the dark. You will need to deal with your emotions and I will need to deal with mine. We will survive, maybe even better. Tell Kelly I'm alive, in case the subject comes up. Good-bye..." Silence. I hung up the phone.

All through my life I worried about one thing or another, one person or another, one day, the next, past, present, future. I have been living in the line of anger, hate and abuse of other people and in the shadows of guilt, fear and shame of my own emotions and I don't know why. I have emotions that I cannot name tormenting my days and haunting my nights. Where do they come from? Do other people have them, too? Do other people ask these questions?

Other people...other people...other people!

I gave myself three weeks to learn or forget or both. I don't need to figure things out in one night!

The room smelled of tobacco and greasy fried foods. The light bulb was shrouded in a thin layer of gray smoke film, I noticed as I reached up to switch off the light. My last thought was of the booze I left behind at home. How unlike me not to pack any. Then, I must have fallen asleep.

I woke up to sounds around me. Strange sounds. Unfamiliar sounds. I was disoriented:

'Where am I?' A thin ray of sunlight poured through a tiny hole in a tear of the drapery.

'Oh, no, he's going to talk about that damn bird again!' I thought.

'No, that was yesterday. I'm not at home.'

'That's right. I'm at Tom's place.'

'That's right. What am I doing here, anyway? I'm alone. Well, that's a good sign! I remember now, I ran away from home! Today is already tomorrow! I made it through a night, all alone! Thank you, God! Life is already changing and all I did was sleep. No, things are not going to be the same when I return!'

I gave the T'bird a full tank of gas for breakfast, grabbed a donut and a styrofoam cup full of black coffee, orange juice. 'Maybe one more donut.' I pointed the T'Bird's beak toward East.

'Onward little soldier, onward.' I pushed all the buttons needed for the luxury drive of the late 80's. Climate control, auto pilot, Dolby stereo sound...we've come a long way since inventing the wheel!

Less than ten miles and it started up again. Emotions! Tightness in my chest and stomach, pounding in my head and heart! My entire body began to tremble.

"Oh, God, are you busy?" I was afraid. I was panicking! From what? Something inside of me. Certainly not from anything outside. Images of my childhood criss - crossing, speeding, flashing through my mind. Not visions but images. I saw them in my mind, not in front of my eyes. My body broke out in a sweat. I had a strong need to vomit. I quickly pulled to the side of the road, threw the gear shift into park and ran for the grassy ditch.

'Well, it's one way to recycle a continental break-fast,' I thought. I felt better. Back in my car there was a dialogue waiting for me:

'So what are you going to do when you get to New York?'

'I'll find out when I get there.'

'Thirteen years of living in that city and you didn't have enough?'

'I'll visit some people. Maybe my ex-in-laws.'

'You nuts? Where will you stay at? In Central Park?'

'I'll call my friend Perry. Yeah! That's right! He'll fix me up.'

'At last! Now we're getting somewhere. Probably the best idea you had in two days. Better get back on the road.'

"On the road again...I can't believe I'm on the road again..." I began to hum. I drove all day long. I couldn't remember my thoughts, time just flew by. When my awareness returned, it was dark again. End of day two. Yeah, Tom and his lights were waiting for me. Des Moines, Iowa. There was a liquor store near the motel.
I purchased a different god to worship: Mr. Brandy.

From my room I called my friend Perry in New York. Everything was fine. I had a place to stay while in the Big Apple. I broke open the seal of the brandy bottle and filled

23

the milky white plastic cup to the rim. I downed it in one continuous drink.

"Sorry God, I didn't promise anything." I don't remember if the room smelled of tobacco or greasy fried foods. I didn't care if there was a gray smoke film shrouding the light bulb. I never switched it off. I had no emotions or thoughts of anything. The brandy burned its way into and through my cells. It was a silent night both outside and inside. I don't remember if I fell asleep or passed out.

I woke up to the sun high in the sky and a drumbeat loud in my head. I was dehydrated and ached all over. Things were back to normal. Hm. Youngstown, Ohio. Called my friend Perry, he was waiting for me. Called my husband, he wasn't. I didn't eat or drink. I went to bed looking forward to the meaningful smile of my friend. I fell asleep from exhaustion and burning up my energy in expectation.

Chapter 3

The City of Stone and Drama

Left my car parked at the curb on East 59th Street. I jumped up the five front steps of the old brownstone building and with a shaking finger I pushed the bell button to announce my presence.

"...be right down!" The intercom crackled. It has been five years since I've seen Perry in the South Pacific, during my *princess* days. Have I changed much? Any? He scooped me up into his arms and I wrapped mine around his neck. I started to cry immediately.

"Damn, I knew I should have gone to the bathroom first, maybe I'd be out of liquid by now!" Bad joke, but we both laughed. He carried my battered suitcase and I carried my battered body up the flight of stairs. Inside the tiny apartment the table was set for two, with a soft, lazy flicker of a candlelight coming from a stem stuck into an empty wine bottle. 'Decidedly more cozy than Tom's place. Cheaper, too.' Perry closed the door behind us and handed me a glass of wine.

"If I remember correctly, you preferred Chardonnay?" My friend looked at me. Yes, he remembered correctly. Of course nowadays *alcohol* would have been a much more accurate word.

"I bet you need one of these, after this trip." He continued on. "Woman, you must be crazy wanting to drive all the way here, alone!"

I smiled and at that moment I figured out the difference between *want* and *need.* I didn't need the wine, but wanted it. I didn't want to drive all alone, but needed to. How right my friend was - I was crazy. Conversation went slow between us. Testing words, feeling out each other's minds, intentions. Five years left a breath of break in closeness, even if short lived.

"So, you finally decided to leave your husband, huh?" he commented. I didn't know I was doing that.

"Well..." was all I had a chance to utter.

"I can't believe you stuck it out with him for this long. How many years now? Ten?"

"Well, only nine," I defended my marriage. As if he didn't hear me, he kept on.

"What life must have been for you to live with such a cold fish! You know, everyone on the Island talked about you two. We couldn't figure out the attraction between the two of you!" Perry spoke his thoughts.

"It's been difficult..." I broke into my daily cry. This time I gave it my all. It was a boiling volcano from deep within finally building to the top, to the rim and over the edge, bursting into an eruption of unrestrained flow of emotions launched for freedom. My tears felt hot and endless as they streamed down my cheeks, like molten lava out of control. I sobbed and sobbed, cleansing, releasing long forgotten, buried emotions still unnamed. Perry sat down next to me. Patiently and silently he began stroking my hair. There was nothing sexual in his touch. I sensed more nurturing in his simple strokes than I had received from any man throughout my lifetime. His friendship puzzled me for a second. For the most part I just let go. He asked for nothing in return for the gentle caring he gave me. That also puzzled me, much longer than a second.

Having exhausted all my energy, I finally stopped sobbing and sighing. Perry was still quiet. Then, he stood up, bent over and lifted me off of the chair and carried my body into his own bedroom. Ever so carefully he lay me into the center of his bed and pulled the covers over me.

"I'd like to stay next to you until you fall asleep. Unless you want me to go. I am your friend and I love you." The tenderness in his voice reassured me.

"Please..." was all I said, leaving him the final choice. He planted a whisper of a kiss on my left shoulder, then lay next to me atop the covers and I fell fast asleep. It could not have been past 6:00 PM on Sunday evening.

There was music coming from the kitchen when I awoke. I saw the daylight filter through the venetian blinds hanging over the tall window of the New York Brownstone. I knew where I was at. Still in the center of the bed my friend gave up for my rest, under the covers, wearing the clothes I had traveled in the day before. Safe. As I turned my head, I noticed a handwritten note propped up against the telephone. It read:

"You are the first woman to have slept in that bed! This is the perfect time to call me." I smiled and dialed his work number.

"The city of Stone and Drama. Your old Brownstone and my old Drama," I said as I heard his voice at the other end of the line.

"Imagine that, and you've only just begun." I could feel his smile across the wires. How correct he was. Perry was a tall man, way over 6 feet. I was stretching for 5' 6". He liked taking walks through the city, for whatever reason I couldn't figure out. Next to his lazy strides I was a galloping pony, forever trying to catch up. We had fun. We walked and laughed and talked and talked and talked. He did not ask questions, yet he was interested. He was my friend. When I asked him something, he replied honestly. Often, he gave me answers I didn't like hearing. Still, I knew that his intentions were kind. It was not what he said, but how I perceived what he said that made the difference. With or without intention, Perry taught me the meaning of perception. I paid attention. We respected each other.

Intention, attention, perception. 'Where are all these words coming from? I haven't read anything meaningful in years, save for some art books!' I thought.

Two, three days passed. We relaxed. He went to work and I stayed at his Brownstone with the five front steps. He made no attempt to be physical or sexual with me.

In the past, I would have been clawed over and over by now, by other men. I felt safe. I felt secure. I'd let go. There was a brief but strong moment once, when I thought 'What if I didn't go back?' Deep inside my mind I knew not to complicate my already chaotic life any farther.

Some of those unnamed emotions began to surface again, mostly during the times when I walked in the park. Strange. There was something stirring somewhere in my stomach whenever I spotted a little girl with her father or father image, as they played together. I became anxious and had to leave the park and the sight of them. When I mentioned it to Perry, his response was completely surprising:

"Have you ever heard of hypnosis?"

"Of course I have. You volunteer to go up on the stage and some man in a black suit and funny hat makes you cluck like a chicken."

"No!"

"Fine. How about, the same man says something to you, then you start gyrating your pelvis and start singing, believing you are Elvis? People in the audience laugh at you like crazy, the man snaps his fingers, you shake your head not remembering a thing?"

"You win" said Perry, "some do, yes. But a professional hypnotherapist can get you to remember. Remember things from your past which otherwise you can not. You can find out about your memories, fears, allergies, headaches, why you cry so much...all kinds of stuff." Perry went on testing my receptiveness.

"You can find out the real reason why you need to cry so often as you do."

"Do I wanna know? What if its something terrible?" I asked.

"Then he can make you look at that terrible thing in a different way so it won't be bad anymore."

"You kiddin' me. You mean he can change what happened to people?"

"No! He can only get you to see and interpret what happened differently." He was getting anxious.

"Oh," was all I said.

"So where would you like to go on your birthday?" I asked him. It was coming up on June 1st and to me right about now was the perfect opportunity to get away from my past and into his future.

"The Rainbow Room."

"You crazy? I ain' got that kind o' money!"

"You asked."

He had been the provider for all of my twenty four- hour needs for the past ten days. That evening I made reservations for two at the Rainbow Room. I arranged for a white stretch limo, also. He managed to get two tickets to the 'Phantom of the Opera' at the Majestic Theater with Michael Crawford performing.

Perry celebrated his thirtieth birthday with a friend. Me.

July, 1965. New York Worlds Fair.   Seventeen years old and one hundred and eighty pounds.

Chapter 4

Carla

*"Surrender yourself to the Divine and invite its
loving power to fill you and you will experience
a miracle of your own making."*
L. Manonne Fontainne

There was another person I wanted to see while in New York. Her name is Carla. She was from Asmara, Ethiopia, Africa. I met her in 1970, nearly twenty years before. We both spoke a definite broken English at that time, yet understood each other perfectly.

"Hey, bud, gotta minute?" I questioned Perry.

"Bored?" He asked back.

"No, tomorrow I'm going to see another friend."

"You got two friends? Lucky Lady!"

"I have known this woman for nearly twenty years. She's a Spiritualist Priestess from Africa. A long time ago I belonged to her assembly or church or temple or call it what you like."

"Yeah? Get out o' here! Want to tell me about it?" He was curious.

"Not sure how much there is to tell or even how to tell. Some people thought she's kind of a witch and stuff. But I knew better."

"You did."

"Yeah. A long time ago I had a lump in my breast and she taught me how to make it go away."

"You serious?" Perry asked.

"I am. She took me into this room in her house. There was no furniture in it, only pillows. Lots o' pillows. Pillows and flowers. And some weird music. We both sat on the floor with our legs crossed. Like when you meditate, you know? Then she told me to close my eyes and listen to her breathing and breathe like her. I did. Then she talked to me about how God can and does take care of everything big or small, good or bad. All I needed to do is believe it. "Believe it and you'll see it," she said. Then she told me to put my right hand onto my breast where the lump was and hold my left palm facing up to the sky and imagine that there is a beautiful shaft of golden light coming through the roof of the building, all the floors above us, the ceiling and into my palm. And that golden light then goes up my arm, into my shoulder, across my back, into my right shoulder, right arm, right hand and into the spot where the lump in my breast was located. I struggled with it, thinking: 'I'm gonna get zapped by some unseen electrical current this woman is woo-dooing into me.' Finally I said to her:

"I can't see the golden light, Carla."

""Why not?" she asked me.

"Because there isn't one. I can't see one."

"Can you see God?" she asked.

"No."

"Do you believe in God?" She asked again.

"Well, now you see, I'm not sure." I wasn't.

"There is your problem, Sugar. You don't believe in God, you can't see the light."

"Oh." I thought it was the end of it.

"Sugar, open your eyes. Now look at me. What am I doing?" At that point she began to dramatically inhale and exhale.

"You are breathing, silly!" I told her somewhat annoyed.

"What am I breathing?"

"Carla, trust me, you are breathing air."

"How do you know? Can you see air?" I had an urge to slap her.

"Well," I said "with all the pollution and stuff..."

"Don't try to be cute, Sugar. I am making a point here. Can you see the air I am breathing in?" She was soft spoken.

"No," I said, treating her with more respect. "No, I can't."

"But you know that there is air even though you cannot see it."

"Yes."

"How did it get there?"

"You gonna tell me?" I was being a wise...? again.

"God put it there. God is everywhere, you need only to consciously pull him into your thinking mind. God makes everything. God is good." She finished and I started up.

"If God can do all that and God is so good, then why do I have to have a lump in my breast? I'm only twenty three years old! Is there a bad God, too?" An unexpected anger flared up inside of me.

"No, Sugar. There is only one God and God is good." She nearly whispered now. "He didn't put the lump there."

"Oh no? Who did?"

"You did, child."

"You crazy!" I jumped up off the floor.

"Sit down. Listen. God cannot make anything bad. God gives us the freedom to choose and make our decisions from all those choices. You were lonely. You wanted attention. You made a lump. You got attention."

"You got a lot o' nerve! I'm outta here!" I jumped up again heading for the door, this time downright mad!

"Come back here, Sugar. Sit down before you wear yourself out. I returned once again, to hear what else she could say to annoy me.

"Things are not always as they seem. Much of the things we believe in we had learned from our parents and people around us. They learned to believe what they were taught by those before them. Generations before generations.

"What about books?" I asked her.

"I'll get to that later," she answered me softly and peacefully.

"You see, Sugar, to a person who is color blind everything is either dark or light gray, maybe black. To you a color is more than just gray. To you each color has a shade and tint and intensity. Everything is as how we individually perceive things."

"How do you know so much. You didn't even go to high school!" I was cynical and cruel.

"God teaches me."

"I should a' guessed! When?"

"All the time. Everywhere. Day and night."

"How?"

"I have learned to listen," said Carla kindly.

"God really talks to you?"

"God talks to everybody and everything all the time. We just don't listen. Let's say there is a class at school with a very nice teacher. Half of her students listen to her teachings the other half does not. Which half do you think will learn her teachings? Or let's say there is a person who is very generous and gives gifts freely to people she doesn't even know. She just hands her gifts out to strangers on the street. Some people will take her gifts believing that she is wonderfully generous, yet other people will walk by her thinking she has lost her mind. Now tell me, who is right and who is wrong?"

"It all depends on how you look at it?" I was not about to make a decision.

"Exactly!" She exclaimed.

"You can be a believer or a skeptic of the very same thing. It's all up to you. It's a choice, Sugar, it's a choice." She patted my hands and asked:

"Wanna close your eyes?"

"O.K."

"So, what happened?" Perry became intensely curious.

"I went to see her every day for six weeks. I wasn't sure about much yet, but I believed in her. In the seventh week, as I had a check up, my doctor shook his head in disbelief and said:

"I don't know how, but it's gone. It's completely gone!! Can't find it. Don't understand it, really." I smiled and kept silent. Somehow I knew that his scientific mind would not comprehend how the *Golden Light from God's hand* with the help of a woman from Africa guided me to re-create my own health."

"I did not stop seeing Carla. In fact, on December 4th, 1973 she became a Priestess of the Temple of the Golden Light and I was initiated into the Sisterhood of that congregation. The only white woman in it, at that time! She lived and still lives in the Bronx. She became my teacher and guide for Spiritual Healing. I used to be able to touch people, go into a relaxed state of mind and make their pain go away. But, after I got married, my husband forbade me to do it. He said it was Anti-Christian and witchcraft. I guess you are supposed to believe in people you love, so I quit doing it. It's been fifteen years since I had seen her. Anyway, I'm going to visit her tomorrow. Wanna come?"
I ended my story in a question.

"No, thanks." Perry declined gracefully.

I had spent only that first night in Perry's bed. The rest of the nights I slept on a foldout futon he had in the tiniest living room I ever had seen. Who needs a lot of room when you get along?

I switched off the little reading light and as I made my tiny nest for the night, I wondered:

'If God could heal my body then, could he heal whatever was hurting so bad, so deep inside of me now, I cannot reach for it?'

"Our Father, who arte in Heaven....For Thine is the Kingdom and the Power and the Glory....Now and Forever. Amen."

Perry bent over and planted a soft kiss atop my forehead. Then, he stood up and headed for his own bed in the other room.

"You are quite something, you know that? Yeah. You are my best friend. Good night, Sugar," he said before halfway closing the door to his room. He turned just enough so I could see a little smirk of a smile on his face.

"Good night, Perry." I really wished then, that we were more than just 'friends'.

Everything was as I remembered. The basement was still damp from the cold winter months. Smoky haze lingered in horizontal layers from the burning of incense. There was one window available to look out of, in case someone needed to determine the time of day. Time did not exist here. The large room was filled with people sitting on old, worn-out metal kitchen chairs displaying yellowed foam padding through the cracks in their vinyl coverings. All was orderly and very, very clean. Men and women sat quietly and smiled at me as I stepped down into the room. I automatically smiled, not so much in returning their warm greetings, rather, because I recalled the feelings I once had here. All those long, fifteen years ago. I took an empty chair and sat on it. I had a while to wait. I closed my eyes, folded my hands into my lap, my head lowered. 'I feel calm here. Peaceful.' Feelings of love and tenderness filled me. How I loved this woman! Those feelings never went away, only got buried under the accumulations of life's daily trash. Hm. 'How did I ever wander off my path? When?'

"You could be a great healer!" Carla once said to me. "But first, you must heal yourself." Well, I didn't get to do either.

A door, which I didn't notice before, suddenly swung open and an ample body covered in a long purple dress virtually whirled, like a purple tornado, directly in front of me. She stopped, took my head in both her hands and pressed it against her ample chest. As expected, I immediately began to cry.

'She recognized me!' I thought. 'All those many years and she still recognized me!' When she let go, we looked into each other's eyes. I saw a tear escape her lid, innocently rolling down her cheek.

"I knew you were close. I didn't sleep much in the last twelve days. I knew you'd come. I felt it. I knew it! Don't go away! I'm busy now but don't go away!" Those were Carla's first words to me and I wouldn't have moved for the world!

For two and a half hours I sat in that chair remembering, visualizing, feeling as people came and went. When there was no one left but me, Carla walked out of her room in a much less dramatic fashion. We embraced each other. There was much more of her to hug now than fifteen years ago!

"How are you?" She asked and I laughed out loud at her question.

"Within twenty some people around me in this room you've *sensed* that I am here and now you're asking how I am?"

"In a lot of pain," she answered seriously.

"Yes. In a lot of pain." I agreed.

After informing Perry of my intention to stay with Carla, I spent the next two nights and days with her and her alone. She opened me up to God again and unleashed the invisible bondage of my spirit. She taught me to really let go, to accept and love unconditionally. She taught me how to trust all over again, to believe and live in the present moment. She assured me that God's purpose is always

Divine and that all negativity is made by men and men's ego. She showed me how to believe in the abundant potential of everything that there is, including mine. And once again, she and I set down on the floor of that very same room, face to face. We closed our eyes and she began to breathe and I followed her guidance. I grab-held of the golden light and pulled it into my heart, into my mind, into all of my cells. In the silence we listened to God. I heard God say:

"Everything is as it need to be. You are where you need to be. Listen to your heart and follow your dreams. There are no mistakes, only mistaken choices. You have much healing to do. Believe in me, everything is as it need to be. Be still...and know that I am God."

She told me how the world and the entire Universe is a living thing and how it is growing and changing. She told me about Earth's changes and my place in the real world: in the Kingdom of God.

" Sugar, don't confuse God with religion. Believe in all the things you cannot see, because some other creature of God's might. Listen in the silence to sounds you cannot hear. Listen with your heart and your spirit. Forgive whoever you believe has wronged you and you will be free of the burdens of judging them in hatred. Don't ask God to forgive you, child, he can't. *God has never judged you.* Forgive yourself for having all those hurtful thoughts, ambitions, actions. Let go of them and ask God to fill up the new and empty spaces with himself. Ask God to lead you...but follow him. Ask God to speak to you...but listen. Ask God to teach you...but learn. Ask God to be with you...but let him in. Ask and you shall receive."

"Carla, do you know that I never read the Bible?"

"So," she shrugged her shoulders, "one day you will. A book is a book" she went on. "All knowledge comes from God. People who write books gather information and knowledge from other books which other people had written before them and so on. Who wrote the first book ever? I'd like to meet that person! Where did he get his information and knowledge from? God. Everything comes from the same source. People don't invent things nor do they discover anything. They simply uncover what had already been there for eons. Everything is revealed in its own perfect time and place. She looked deep into my eyes.

"So who wrote the first book?" I asked her jokingly.

"God did. Someone was listening as God was dictating." She smiled sweetly.

"You have an answer for everything!"

"No. Only to those things which God reveals to me."

"I think I'll buy a Bible tomorrow."

"Forget tomorrow, why not start with the Book of Psalms now?" She handed me a small book in a light green cover. I accepted it.

"So, do you want to read my cards?" I asked her, wishing she would.

"No" she said. "God will tell you all you need to know. Listen, child. Listen." I kept sitting on the floor. I was draped in a blanket of peace and calmness. I was sure God draped it over me and I didn't dare disturb it.

Time rushed by too fast and I had to leave New York.

"I don't want to go, though I know that I must." I was pained at our parting.

"By the time you arrive, you'll be glad you're there. Much changes are ahead for you. Changes are often painful and you will experience pain like never before. The process of letting go will hit you from all directions. Remember this clearly: it is not always important that you understand what is happening around you. Simply be aware of them. Ask, be open to receive and you will. *God never closes a door before he opens another.* Call me if your pain becomes too much. The times when we think that we are the only living creation on Earth are the times when we don't reach out and ask. *We are always, yet never alone.*" Then she said:

"Sugar, go and see the man who will put the light on your past. He ain't gonna make you cluck like no chicken."

"How do you know about that?" I asked her in shock.

"I love you, that's how."

Chapter 5

The Return

Throughout my life, I cultivated a presence which was not very deserving. Worthless. Most of the people in my life - past and present - thought of me worthless. Not all, most. Well, plenty some. It's not their fault. I had trained them to. Things, beliefs, life will have to change. I had been back at home from New York for two months. Either no one noticed any changes in me or didn't know how to let me know that they had noticed. At times I wondered if they even notice that I had returned! Life goes on. Again.

One day in August my daughter decided that she was moving out. She was already twenty one and had a baby of her own, so I thought it was a good thing. After they left the house became a huge place for two people who did not communicate with each other. My husband and I.

I moved out of our bedroom to a lower level room of our house, to my husband's surprise and displeasure. He and I barely talked to each other by then and when we did, it was more like him complaining more and more about me. I took a serious interest in our businesses against his wishes. He kept telling me that people, our employees were very upset by my presence and that everyone hated me. It sounded as though my changing didn't help our lives. He thought I best stay home.

Sometime in early September, I suggested to him that we go to see a marriage counselor. He declined but strongly recommended that I do seek help, so I found a psychologist who was well known for being a caring professional. When I told him my news he nearly hit the roof: "Did you have to get the most expensive one!"

"Gee, sorry! I didn't know I could get one at a garage sale!" I shouted back at him.

At the end of my first appointment the doctor determined that I was sick enough to see him twice a week! Through a multiple question test he summed me up to be very ill: an alcoholic, chemically dependent suicidal manic depressive and a schizophrenic paranoid. He made an appointment for me to see another doctor for medications. I was back on drugs, legal though as they were! Lithium and Prozac. For three weeks I took my pills and my self to sit in his chair, rehashing the miseries of my marriage and whatever else there was in life. I didn't feel any better. In fact, I felt worse. At the end of the third week the doctor's secretary phoned me at my office:

"I wanted to call you in person as soon as I could, just so you won't hear it from someone else, first. Dr. John will not be able to see you any longer." Said the voice on the phone.

"I see, why is that?" I asked her.

"Sorry Manonne, but Dr. John committed suicide. He hung himself on a tree."
I felt as though life stopped in me, also.

Our whole town was in shock to hear the news and rumors of his possible motives were everywhere. My husband, of course, had the only logical answer:

"He was a perfectly capable doctor until you went to see him. He had to kill himself just to get away from you!" It was a terrible thing to say to a person who was trying desperately to get well, even as a joke. Was he joking?

I got drunk that night. After four months of healing, I got drunk. Really drunk!

Months before, Carla had said to me:

"One person alone cannot make a 180 degree turn and have everything else around them stay the same. Everything in your life will have to change. When you see a worm in an apple still on the tree, you had better spray the entire tree to get rid of the pests. Spraying a single apple

42

just wont do."   She had often surprised me with her parallels.

I struggled with time and Mr. Brandy, some Mr. Gallo, too.

"You should read more" said my husband. "You are not very aware of what's going on in the world!"

"O.K." I answered him. "What do you suggest I read?"

"You waste a lot of money buying these magazines on decorating and stuff. You should get more serious about finances, since you're still going to the office. Maybe you should even consider taking some classes at the college. A little more education wouldn't hurt you!"

"You know, you are should-ing all over me?" My husband looked at me, surprised:

"What did you say?"

"I want you to stop should-ing all over me!"

"You said: 'should', right?"

"Yes, I did."

"Oh, O. K. I thought you used another word."

"Isn't that the same thing?"

"Well, it's just a word," he shrugged.

"No it isn't! *It's an attitude*. I want to sell this house and buy two separate ones. One for you and one for me. I cannot live with you any longer."

"What? Have you lost your mind? Do you have any idea how much stuff we'll have to divide? What will people think?" He spoke his truth. I could not believe what I just heard. On second thought yes, I could.

"You don't have to worry about how and what to divide. I'll take the antique store and gallery, a small house near downtown and my car. I want the house paid for, however. As for people - they will think that we no longer get along and we are on our way to get a divorce. Of course, you may tell them whatever you wish."

"You are serious about this, aren't you?"

"Like my life depends on it!" I said. It did.

"Hello, this is Kathy" the voice introduced its owner.

"Hello Kathy, I am Manonne. You were recommended to me by the National Guild of Hypnotists. I understand that you are an experienced therapist in regression. I need to make an appointment with you as soon as possible." I was very nervous and spoke rapidly.

"What do you believe your need is?" she asked.

"Well, you see, I have this addictive personality and I must find out what causes it. You think you can help me?"

"It's up to you," she said. "Therapy is 90% subject and 10% therapist."

'Why must everything always be up to me? There just isn't any easy way out!' I thought.

"I understand." I said. "When can you see me?"

Two weeks later I was laying in a comfortable green leather recliner, wondering what in the world am I doing there. 'Am I a chicken now or will I be one later?' I thought jokingly. Kathy did not look the part of what I expected, whatever that was. She was a simple, slim woman in a simple, purple dress. Short brown hair, glasses, smelling sweet like vanilla. Instead of jewelry, she wore a bright and expensive smile. She didn't offer her hand in greeting, instead came straight toward me with her arms opening to hold me in a friendly hug. I couldn't help but smile back at her. She then stepped back and bowed her head with her hands pressed together in front of her face. Hm.

She asked me question after question about myself, my fears, my general health and what I really wanted. When she was done questioning, she assigned me to complete a few childish tasks and got me back onto the green recliner.

"Open your eyes... now close them...relax...open your eyes...now close them again... relax... relax... relax... relax... you will be aware of everything around you...inside of this room...as well as the outside..." I heard the tape recorder click on.

Five and a half hours later I heard her voice again, crystal clear:

"You feel refreshed, relaxed, vital and bursting with new energy as if you had just awaken from a full night's sleep. You chose to remember every detail of this session and you will. In fact, each day will bring more and more details of your life's experiences, which are related to this session, into focus. You will be remembering the truth of these experiences, without emotions or physical feelings. Do you have any questions at this time?"

"No." I heard my voice say.

"You are now ready to open your eyes. When I snap my fingers you will be fully alert and in your natural state of consciousness, feeling better than you have ever felt throughout your entire life." Snap! My eyes opened. I was there and awakened. Seemed to be alive, also.

"Manonne," she said "look at me, who am I?"

"Hm...a...the chicken lady." I answered her lazily and yawned.

"Huh? Manonne, who am I?" She seemed worried.

"You are Kathy. You are my therapist." I assured her.

"What year are we in?"

"1989."

"Good," she relaxed. "How are you feeling?"

"Hm...I'm not sure. I feel light. Yes, I feel kind of light. Lazy, too!"

"Good."

I stretched and yawned again. I felt incredibly relaxed, as if I were on some kind of drug again. No, not like that. Better! Different! I felt wonderful!

"Listen to me," she interrupted my thoughts. "Lots of things came up. Things which you have buried into deep chambers of your subconscious mind for most of your life. Things which you will need to deal with, accept and let go of in your conscious life. We will need to spend much more time together to have you heal completely. You have only just begun." said Kathy.

"Yes, I know." I assured her. I thought: 'No matter where I turn I seem to be always just beginning. When will I at least get a few steps ahead?'

"Now that you have started, it is important to continue," she went and I wondered if she picked up on my own thoughts.

"I know."

"Do you want to continue now?"

"No. I have to digest this whole thing first!"

"I understand." She did. "Take this number, it's my home phone. Call me anytime, day or night, if things get out of control. Can you see me in two days?" She was persistent and later on I fully understood why.

"O.K." The relaxation began to fade away and I wanted to leave.

"Manonne, much more of your memory will come back in your dreams and reveal things which you are not consciously aware of, yet. Flow with it. They cannot hurt you now, not ever. They are just memories. They are not happening to you now. You have already lived and survived through all of them. You are a winner. Don't shove them back down again. Let them flow freely. Let all feelings, thoughts, memories, everything pass." She sounded a lot like Carla. It comforted me. I left Kathy's office.

I sat in my car in the parking lot for a long time. God, she was right! Lots of stuff came up. More to come. How much more? Flow with it! We tapped into the river of my past and now it's open to flow freely. I drove home as quickly as I could before the flood gates opened. I had six sixty minute tapes in my purse.

'Was I really hypnotized for all that time? I had to have been to get all this garbage out! Don't be afraid. All emotions pass...'

Once in my home, I went directly to my studio to lock the tapes away. I sat down, silently, without a thought. When Carla's sweet face flashed into my mind I began to breathe her rhythm:

"I am calm. I am relaxed. I am in control..."

"Forgive them and your own burdens will be lifted. Forgive yourself for punishing yourself for those things which are beyond your control. Forgive." Carla's voice echoed in my mind. How did she know?

The following two nights and days I did not sleep. Since I lived and functioned pretty much alone in our house by this time, there were no domestic disturbances or even questions. No one knew, no one cared.

From time to time I asked my husband if he listed our house on the real estate market. He did. No interested buyers, so I left it at that. For the most part I painted. My art work was selling well. I took full charge of the gallery and antique store and supported myself pretty nicely. There was no question in my mind that we were done with our marriage, so I went on planning for the future alone - in case there was a future.

Kathy and I grew closer after each of our sessions.
I saw her professionally for over two months, a total of seventeen times. At first twice, then once a week. It is largely because of her that this book came to life. Do to her constant encouragement and support I became a hypnotherapist myself and it is because of her urgings, combined with Carla's faith in me that I chose the path of a minister and spiritual healer. There is nothing in the world I'd rather do now!

Carla and Kathy have never met. Each woman comes from a different background from the other.

Carla, from a war ridden, savaged country in Eastern Africa. She herself, a child of a raped mother left behind to guide and scarcely provide for her fatherless, 'sin - conceived' child. She proudly sported her six grade education which was higher that most children of her generation received. Through her deep, spiritual convictions she had the ability to patiently and lovingly open up more doors to the knowledge of my inner mind than most of the trained educators had try to during the years of my formal education.

Kathy grew up in a loving, well balanced and highly educated family of Northwestern heritage. She herself is well balanced, highly educated and deeply spiritual. Worlds apart, the two women are nearly identical and truly Angels on Earth.

Chapter 6

On Memory Lane

"God, I am nothing without you: I surrender to you
My body, my mind and my spirit.
Fill me with yourself and with you within me,
Moment by moment, I am the best that I can be."
L. Manonne Fontainne

"Hello, I am Manonne and I once was an alcoholic. I also have an addictive personality. It used to be my prison. Today it is my blessing."

I cannot remember between my earliest memory and the age of forty four when I was not drinking something alcoholic. I was born into a family where infantile pain was not permitted. From the time I discovered crying, I was quickly and effectively eased out of my misery, by some member of my family easing some wine or plum liquor into my milk bottle. I went through colic, diaper rashes, teething, the terrible twos and all forms of banging and bruising while happily and actively boozing. I don't know if it was a national culture, but certainly it was our family culture.

While I was at home it was natural to me. As I grew older and attended schools away from home it became apparent that I was already addicted to alcohol. Yet, it was only a fraction of my sicknesses. Suffice to say that feeding alcohol to an infant is an abusive act, my family's abuse did not end there. As I listened to those six tapes over and over again for nearly a year and worked my way into a better mental and emotional health, I wondered with genuine concern, just how many other children had there been and still are out there, whose lives are being shaped by unwell, dysfunctional adults.

As I asked you at the beginning of this book, I ask you once again: "Have no judgment, hate or anger. I have none. I am totally blessed and I feel grateful for every moment of my life's experiences."

Tape number one was the most difficult to listen to, though Kathy programmed my subconscious mind to view every detail from a distance as an observer, rather than a participant. I had and still have no emotions about any of my recollections. She has revised all of my perceptions to a new, healthy and acceptable interpretation of each event. The greatest service any hypnotherapist can provide for their clients!

After regressing my conscious mind to the proper level of depth, Kathy aided me to visualize a bridge. I was to walk across this bridge. This was the bridge of my own life and on each side, left and right of this bridge there were the years, months, weeks and days of my life's experiences. I was passing through and beyond these experiences. She, then suggested that at the end of this bridge there is a very large field. This is the field where I had in my spirit or subconscious mind first experienced a feeling that there is something unnatural happening to me. This could be at any age, at any time with or without any persons involved. She suggested that I will not reach this memory until I reach the very end of the bridge. When the true memory is clear I would be at the end of the bridge and ready to step off, able to give her a report on what is happening in the memory. I would have no feelings of any kind. I would simply and easily give her a report. When I arrived at the memory, I'd give her a signal by raising my index finger on my left hand. That's it. After a time - I don't know how long - I did.

"Very good, Manonne. You are doing great! Tell me, are you inside or outside?"

"Bent vagyok..." I said.

"Very good Manonne. I want you to use your Divine Intelligence and hear me, understand me and answer me

50

with your knowledge of the English language. The language, which you are now using in your current, natural life in 1989. Are you willing to do that?" She recovered instantly from the surprise reply I provided to her first question, which was not in English.

"Yes..."

"Very good, Manonne, thank you. Once again, are you inside or outside?"

"Inside..."

"Is it daytime or nighttime?"

"Daytime..."

"Are you alone or are you with other people?"

"With other people..."

"Look around yourself and tell me the year of this experience."

"I don't know the year..."

"How old are you now, Manonne?"

"I am in my third month of life..."

"Are you a baby?"

"Yes..."

"Tell me, is it hot or cold inside, where you are at?"

"I am in bed...it is hot."

"Have you been outside in this life?"

"Yes..."

"Is it hot or cold outside?"

"It is cold..." I was born in the middle of November, so sometime during February in Central Europe must have been the middle of winter. Things were going well.

"What is the name you are being called by at this age?"

"Baba..."

"Thank you," she said. As I listened to her voice on the tape, she sounded as if she may have been smiling. She hesitated then asked her question again:

"May I call you Baba?"

"No..."

"O.K., Manonne. I'd like you now to give me a report of what is happening."

"I am crying...I am hungry...my mother picks me up...I stop crying...I am still hungry...I start crying again...some one is bringing a bottle...she hands it to my mother...it is my grandmother...my mother puts me into my grandmother's arms and she walks out of the room...my grandmother feeds me from the bottle...I hate what's in the bottle..."

"Why do you hate the milk?"

"I need my mother's milk...bottle milk gives me pain in my stomach...my mother has no milk to feed to me...now she does not feed me at all...she gives me away each time I eat...my mother does not love me..."

"Does your grandmother love you?"

"Yes..." said my voice on the tape. "Each time I am in pain I cry...she picks me up and holds me...she is very warm and I can hear her heart beating...I trust her..."

"Do you trust your mother?"

"No..."

"Why is that?"

"She smells funny...she drinks something...it smells sour...sometimes when I cry she puts it into my bottle... instead of milk..."

"Do you know the name of what she puts into your bottle?"

"Yes..."

"Please tell me, what is the name?"

"You call it wine..."

"You are drinking wine from your milk bottle at this age of three months?" Kathy sounded shocked.

"Yes..."

"What happens after you drink the wine?"

"I go to sleep...soon...I don't cry any more..."

"When you are awake, do you cry much?"

"Yes..."

"Why is that?"

"I feel much pain..."

"Where do you feel the pain? In your body?"

"Yes..."

"Where is the pain in your body?"

"In my stomach...my intestines...there is much air inside my body..."

"Where else do you feel pain?"

"In my spirit...no... not there...I feel pain inside...
I, I have no word...it is a need."

"What does it need to make the pain go away?" Kathy asked.

"It needs feeling...it needs love..."

"Don't you receive love?"

"It needs love from my mother...it needs her food..."
I could tell that whatever part of me was communicating with Kathy, it was struggling to be clear and precise. It was also providing answers. Short, little, matter of fact answers. Not at all the way I expressed myself in my natural life.

"Tell me, what is happening right now?" Kathy continued her questioning.

"I am waiting for your instructions..." said the voice on the tape.

"I see. What are you doing in the memory?"

"I am sucking on the bottle of milk my grandmother is holding..."

"Are you laying in bed?"

"No... my grandmother is holding me and feeding me. I already told you..."

"You are correct" said Kathy, surprised at the accuracy of a baby. Or was it a baby who answered her?

"I want you now, to go deep into your Divine Intelligence and find your mother's feelings there.

"My mother came back into the room...she is right here..." the voice interrupted her.

"Thank you for the information. I'd like you now to look into your mother's eyes. Give me a report, what do you see in her eyes?"

"Her eyes are wet...she has been crying...inside, my mother feels much pain...my mother feels guilt...for not having her own milk to feed to me...each time she gives me a bottle, her pain is very strong...she hands me to my grandmother and walks away...my mother wants to love me...she can't...she does...her guilt is too strong..."

"Why does your mother feel this guilt?"

"My mother believes she is void of milk because she drinks alcohol...she drinks alcohol to make her own pain go away..."

"Do you know what her pain is?"

"No...I do not..."

"Thank you, you are doing very well. Tell me Manonne, do you drink much milk in your natural life?" Kathy was on target.

"No...I drink no milk...I am allergic to milk...my body rejects milk..."

"Yes," said Kathy. "All through your life you have associated milk with your mother handing you to someone else. Rejection. You associated milk with rejection. The truth is that your mother felt her own pain for not being able to provide you with her own milk so powerful, that she could not go through with feeding you any other milk. She did not reject you, a beautiful little baby girl, but walked away from her own guilt and pain." Kathy explained. "Can you see that is truth, in her eyes? Can you understand her own pain?"

"Yes..."

"Are you willing to let go of your old belief of your mother's rejection?"

"Yes...I see how much she does want to love me...she smells sour again..."

"Yes. Your mother went out of the room to drink her alcohol and make her own pain go away."

"Her spirit can't make it go away..." said the baby me.

"Forgive her for not feeding you. And forgive yourself for believing that she rejected you and as you forgive, you will be able to drink milk from now on and you will not be allergic to milk any longer.   Do you accept this new understanding as truth?"

"Yes..."

"Do you forgive?"

"Yes..."

"Do you forgive both of you?"

"Yes..."

"When you return to your natural state of awareness, you will, for the rest of your natural life, remember this part of our session lovingly with new understanding and you are going to have a peaceful and compassionate feeling about it."

"I'd like you now to gently allow this memory to fade. Take a deep breath and relax. Again...relax. Very good. One more deep breath and relax. Good." Kathy kept me breathing and relaxing for a while as she kept assuring me how wonderfully safe and secure I was. I believed her. As if she knew I needed to be prepared for what was coming next, she relaxed with me.

"As the memory fades, I'd like you to turn around and face the bridge of your life which is now ahead of you. Begin your memory journey as you live more and more days of your life. You are getting older. Day by day, week by week. You see and remember every day of your life as you walk through it in your memory, just as you were living it right now. "   Kathy's voice came very slowly, softly and quietly through the cassette player. She paused, taking her time, allowing me to see into my memory.

"As you are seeing your life's experiences before you, I'd like you once again, to stop and give me a signal with your index finger on your left hand, when you reach a memory which is unnatural or uncomfortable to you." I did.

"Very good, thank you." Kathy's voice sounded. "Please, give a report. Are you inside or outside?"

"Inside..."

"Is it daytime or nighttime?"

"Daytime..."

"Are you alone or with other people."

"There is one person in the room..."

"Which room are you in?"

"Bedroom..."

"Are you in bed?"

"No...I am in my crib..."

"How old are you at this time?"

"I have lived more than one year...I have not lived two full years, yet..."

"Please give a report, is it cold outside or is it warm?"

"It is both..."

"Are there any flowers outside?"

"Yes..."

"Are there any leaves on the ground?"

"No leaves..."

"Is it springtime?"

"I don't know..."

"Can you play outside?"

"Yes...it is warm enough now..."

"Can you walk, yet?"

"Yes..."

"Can you talk, yet?"

"No..."

"Thank you, you are doing very well. Please give a report, what is happening?"

"I am crying...someone is handing me a bottle..."

"Is it your mother?"

"No..."

"Is it your grandmother?"

"No...this is a man...my mother and grandmother are women..."

"Thank you. Do you know who this man is?"

"Yes..."

"Who is the man?" Kathy was getting tired of the yes and no answers. She soon has changed her style of questioning.

"The man is my uncle..." said my voice.

"Is this uncle a boy, young man, or old man?"

"A young man..."

"Are you drinking from the bottle?"

"Yes..."

"Please tell, what is in the bottle?"

"Wine..."

"Please tell, how often do you drink wine from your bottle?"

"Every day...every time I cry...I am given wine in the bottle..."

"Please tell, why is this day an unnatural one?"

"My uncle brings me the bottle..."

"Please give a report, what is happening?"

"My uncle now picks me up...he sits down onto what you call a sofa...he puts me down onto the floor in front of him...I can stand all by myself now...he lets go of me.. I am holding my bottle in my hands...I am looking up at the ceiling...drinking from my bottle...now my uncle takes it away...he is twisting off the top from the bottle...he is putting something into my bottle...I don't know the name...it is coming out from his pants...he can't put it into the bottle...it is too big...now he is pouring the wine from my bottle onto the...no name...his eyes are closed...now the eyes are open...he is smiling at me...I am smiling at him...he's pulling me closer to him...I am between his legs...he is closing his knees around me...I am very little...he is putting his fingers into my mouth...he is forcing my mouth to open...I open my mouth...his other hand is on the...no name that he was trying to put into my bottle...now he is putting the...no name...into my mouth...it's too big... he is forcing my head closer...I am starting to cry...he slaps my face...I can see that I am hurting...I can see that I am afraid...he jumps up...I can't see the...no name anymore he is twisting the top back onto my bottle...he is putting the bottle into my hands...I am taking my bottle...he is lifting me up...he sits me back in my crib...I am screaming very loud...my mother is in the room...she takes my bottle...she tells my uncle to put more wine into it...I am crying, saying: " Mama...Mama"...my arms are high up in the air...I want her to pick me up...hold me...the bottle is back my hands ...my mother lays me down...puts the bottle into my mouth... I am drinking my wine...still crying...now they are both leaving the room...no one picks me up...drinking my wine stopped crying...I am sleeping..."

"Thank you," whispered Kathy's voice. There was a tremor in that voice coming from the tape player.

Months later, Kathy and I talked about her feelings, her emotions and psychological state about my experiences. My family had affected people far beyond their wildest imaginations.

I was born into a family with more dysfunction than one can ever dream up. I became an alcoholic at a very early age. For every discomfort I felt or thought I had, there was always the bottle. I went through my developing years without developing, without ever naturally and gradually learning to deal with any discomfort: physical, emotional, mental. I did not know how to differentiate between normal and acceptable behavior or dysfunction and I carried this learned behavior into most of my life, including adulthood.

That episode was the first in my regressed memory that surfaced as unnatural, of its kind. The same uncle and I had several other experiences after that one. I was only eighteen months old. He was a pilot and still a very young man when he died in an airplane crash. He left behind his wife, my aunt Irene and an infant little girl who was one year younger than my brother. He must have been in his late twenties and I was around seven years old when he was killed. I did not feel a loss at his death. Today, I understand it more clearly and I am glad for the little girl he left behind. Forty years ago we did not have the counseling available to sex offenders as we do now. Certainly not in Central Europe. I don't know if he would have assaulted his own little girl.
I will never know.

As the months passed by, I learned to walk and run and became very active. We lived at my grandparents' house in one of the two rooms the house had. There was no electricity in the house yet and believe it or not, we still had only dirt floors. Each of the rooms had in it two beds pushed together, filled with a huge hay mattress topped off with a feather bed. I slept between my mother and my father. My father worked during the night at a government bakery and my mother, during the day at a government dry-cleaner. After the second world war everything belonged to the government. My mother would be going to work at just about the time my father was returning home. The commotion would wake me up. Then mommy would leave and daddy'd be coming to bed. I would stay in bed with him until daddy fell asleep, then climb out and go to the kitchen or other room where my grandparents lived. My grandma would fix me breakfast and take care of me. It was a quiet routine. Very quiet.

Daddy taught me to be quiet, to be a good girl and play. He played with me and I played with him. He would throw me up into the air and catch me. Then he would bounce me up and down on his chest...his stomach...then lower down. He would slide me stomach to stomach, up and down...I would be giggling and he'd be making some funny sounds. He played with me like that, often. Just daddy and me. As the weather got warmer, we wore fewer clothes to bed and played more and more. He always told me what a *good girl* I was and he would hold me close to him and he would kiss me all over *and play* with me. Sometimes he'd hurt me...a little...but I loved my daddy. He paid attention to me while my mommy did not. I didn't want to lose my daddy and his love, so I was a very good girl and I played with him. Sometimes I played with him even before he asked me to. After we finished playing, he would hold me close to him and he would tell me how much he loved me and what a good girl I was. Mommy never told me things like that! Oh yes, I would do anything for my daddy!

On my third birthday, as we were playing daddy and I, all of a sudden mommy came home unexpected, interrupting daddy and me. She got sick at the bus stop and decided not to go to work that day. I don't think she liked seeing what she saw! She screamed and started hitting my daddy. When she was done with him, she grabbed me and gave me a beating! I was in such a shock, I never even cried.

The following day she shaved my hair all off! She balded me! She went to buy a little boy's outfit and dressed me in it and began sewing little boys' clothes for me, which she dressed me in until I was five and a half years old when a real boy - my brother was born. I found myself back in the old crib in the kitchen where I listened to my grandfather snore every night. When I asked my mommy why I was no longer sleeping in the big bed, she answered:

"Because you were a very bad girl!"

"But daddy told me I was *a good girl...*" I protested.

"No! You were a very, very bad girl!" My mother yelled. So, whenever I was a good girl to one person I was a bad girl to the other. Was I ever confused! And hurt.

My father's repetitious "*be a good girl and let's play*" training left its mark for years to come, and I had often responded to *good girl* without hesitation, even at those times when I knew that the experience is going to be hurtful and unnatural.

My grandparents had a nice farm, mostly for vegetables and fruits. Not much livestock, some pigs, lots of chickens, ducks and geese. I spent much of my time out in the field, being the only child around. I imitated my grandmother and I would go check on things for her in the field. She taught me much about plants and herbs and weeds and I would help her clear the vegetable beds, learning which one to pull, which plant to save. One day, in the summer of my fifth year of life, one of my grandfather's helpers' son, about thirteen or fourteen years old, came up to me and started to talk to me. He was pulling weeds with me for a little while then suggested that we take a break and play.

"*Be a good girl and let's play,*" he said. On cue, I heard those key words and obliged. He wanted to play very seriously though, because I did not like his game. He made me close my eyes and pulled my panties down. He did not put anything into my mouth. Instead, he pulled my little body close to his and put something warm and hard between my little thighs and kept sliding me up and down. When he was done, he pushed me aside and told me to pull up my panties and open my eyes. He looked at me and said that I was a very bad girl for doing what I did and if I tell anybody what I just did: '*no one will ever love you!*' No one, not even my daddy or mommy! Wow! It worked! I never did say a word to anyone until my memory got recorded on one of those tapes.

He was a smelly boy and I often remembered that smell without the actual experience and had an urge to vomit, even in my later, growing years. I didn't remember him, only that awful smell. Anyway, he left me all alone out in the field. I recalled sitting there under the hot, summer sun. I didn't remember if I cried, nor did I remember any emotions or thoughts I may have had at that time. Only that awful smell. Then my memory recalled my grand -mother's voice calling out my name. I laid down onto the warm ground pretending to be asleep. She woke me up by gently shaking me. We walked home together, my grandma holding my tiny hand in her rough, overworked one. When we got home, I vomited. I kept smelling my clothes and the boy's voice echoed: "No one will ever love your again!" At dinner, without asking, I drank my grandfather's wine. Not once did I ever return to that field all through my life.

Fear was growing strong in me, though. Emotions were growing out of proportion already and I would start to cry for no apparent reason. I had scary dreams. I was too old to have my bottle anymore, so I received my wine in a tin cup. If I didn't, I would throw a tantrum and get my way, eventually. Then, I'd settle down and stop crying, stay quiet and fall asleep. Life was rough for this little four and a half year old. It was remarkable, that I grew up to be as smart and intelligent as I was. I was fantastic! At the age of five I was put into first grade and by the time my brother was born, six months later, I was reading and adding. At the end of the summer I was doing second grade work! My personal life at age five was a mess. Less than six years of age and I was a professional student.

Toward the end of summer 1953, my parents had a party of a sort for my brother's naming. It was his baptismal, but we were not allowed any religion, so they called it: 'naming'. Once again I listened to the familiar *'be a good girl and play'*, this time with my younger cousin.
I guess the adults were ready to get rid of us kids, but were not prepared to learn about my method of playing. I took my cousin by his hand and led him to the back seat of the only car our entire family had and preceded to molest him. I was not yet six and he was only five! When his parents discovered us, they had a surprise. My aunt, in a shock, asked me where I learned to do such things, and I proudly announced, that my daddy taught me. That night I got one of the biggest beatings in my life. From my daddy! He told me that if I ever say that again, he'll kill me! From that day on, my brother became the apple of his eyes and my behind became the target of his belt-beatings. That night my soul gave birth to hate. I nurtured that emotion toward him for the rest of his life and toward most of my family throughout most of my life, except for my grandmother, who had always been and continued to be my only source of solace. And my brother. I had loved his kind spirit.

I was a messed up, used up emotional cripple and academic excellence at age five and a half. Children my age did not want to be with me. I didn't know how to play normal. I was too smart and too scared. My grades were very high and I was pushed fast up into the next level. At less than nine years of age, I was in sixth grade. Still drinking my wine.

Life kept rushing faster and faster into the early winter of 1956. It was a terribly cold fall already, with snow piled on the ground. My parents had a little farm with a tiny house on it. We had just moved into it that summer. I lived there, except for the times I was away at school, until I was seventeen and a half years old. This winter of 1956, I was still eight years old, though my ninth birthday was very near. On this particularly cold October day my mother did not go to work and I was told that there will be no school. There was trouble in the whole country. We had no TV, so we listened to the radio most of the day. Radio Free Europe. Even as a child, I could sense the tension in the house. There was not much talking going on, which was fine with me. Most of the time I was not included in any family conversations, anyway. My job was to go to school, get good grades, take care of my little brother and help out around the house. If something went wrong, I would get a beating from my father. Most of these beatings had very little to do with me, he just beat me because... I am not talking about being spanked, either! He would tell me in the morning that I'm going to get it that night. Then, he would then soak a rope in a bucket of water for the rest of the day, and sure enough I would 'get it' that night! Sometimes he used his belt. Earlier in the day, I would start drinking, so by the time he got hold of my behind, I felt very little pain. I didn't even cry! I just refused to cry, even though he made sure my beatings were received by a naked behind. I could never understand how could he do that to me! I wanted him to love me. I loved him!...I hated him!...I loved him!...I hated him!...I feared him! I hated him!

On this October day in 1956 he was not at home. I wondered if I would get a beating for the trouble in the country, too? As the day progressed, my grandparents and an aunt and uncle with their little girl came to our house. My cousin was very young, only about two or two and a half years old. My family was not well liked by our relatives and I wondered what these people were doing, visiting us. I felt the tension in the adults. We had a cellar under our small, two room house. As the evening drew closer, everyone still remained and had helped to haul most of our blankets, pillows, comforters and warm belongings, plus some immediate food supplies down into the cellar. Half of the cellar was filled with the winter fuel of coal and the dirt floor was as damp and cold as a compacted dirt floor can be. We occupied the other half. There was a small whole in one corner of the ground where my mother stored the harvest of carrots, roots, potatoes and other wintering vegetables. There also sat a huge barrel, filled with homemade wine. I felt safe. We could not burn any coal, for fear that the smoke from the chimney would give our presence away, so we wrapped ourselves in blankets and huddled in the pitch blackness of the cold, October night of 1956 - my grandparents, aunt, uncle and cousin, my mother, my brother and myself.

The Russians overran our small city that night. We were not allowed to even whisper, in fear that our voices might be heard. There was terror all around us, within us! We had no idea of what was going on outside. My brother was three and a half years old. I remember my aunt being pregnant and she must have been pretty far along, because she seemed very uncomfortable. My father was missing from the group, but I did not feel any worry for him. In fact, I remembered that I was somewhat relieved. In later years I thought about this and found my detachment and feelings interesting. I didn't remember how long had we been down there in that cold, damp, dark cellar when I heard footsteps and strange sounding voices outside the house. Then, above us, inside the house I heard furniture thrown around, drawers being yanked and thrown on the floor. Doors were slammed and finally someone was trying to pry open our cellar door! I was petrified! I was afraid that the little ones would make a sound or worse, cry! For some reason, whoever tried could not get into the cellar and the footsteps began to fade away as the sound of crunched snow signaled from a distance and finally disappeared. Then, I heard our animals being disturbed and a cry from a pig I knew was shot. Then another shot, another, another! I gave up counting the gunshots. Time passed. Silence. I couldn't tell just how much time. It could have been an hour, a day, eternity! No more sounds but our own breathing and the echoes of my own heartbeat. I didn't know if it was day or night or morning. We had been locked up into the pitch darkness and dead silence. My aunt became very restless and the children were whimpering. First one and than the other. How did they ever manage to be so quiet all through that time, I could not figure out. But they did. My grandmother held each of them under her arms. My mother sat apart, all by herself next to the wine barrel and I heard my grandpa's breathing from where I remembered the coals to be.

I barely heard, as my mother called out for me and when I answered her, she followed my voice to my side. She sat down next to me on my pillow. She didn't offer to hug me, but she did take my hands into her shaking ones as she began to whisper:

"You are the only one who can fit through the coal-chute. I will lift you up and you will have to climb out and find out what happened. You will have to be very careful, so no one will see you! And you will have to be very, very quiet! *No matter what happens out there, you can't make a sound.* You don't want to frighten the children and make them cry! Now, *be a good girl and go*!" She finished with a warning. I got bundled up in a lot of clothes, some of them not even mine. We struggled with the door of the coalchute, until my grandfather finally forced it open and I got lifted up to it. It was grayish out there, either early morning or dusk. It was bitterly cold and the winter air rushed down, inside. There was a lot of new snow on the ground, that I could see. I stretched my arms up high and pulled myself to the opening. My mother pushed me out the rest of the way. I heard the door fall shut behind me and I jumped at the sound.

I was eight and a half years old, alone and terrified in the cold, white, dead silence. The freezing air hurt my lungs and the whiteness of the snow hurt my eyes. I kept them shut. The light was blinding in the snow, especially after having been locked up for so long in the pitch darkness of that cellar. I kept sitting on the ground with my back against the cold wall of the house. I wanted to die in my fear! There was not a sound to be heard. I was hoping that I might hear some reassuring words from my family below me. Nothing! I felt the warmth of my tears run down my cheeks and I reached up to wipe them away. I kept rubbing my eyes until I slowly dared to open them. I opened and shut them a few times until they began to get used to the light. They hurt in the brightness and blinking helped to get a little view of the immediate world around me. I decided that it was evening time. I had no boots on, but my mother wrapped my feet and legs in layers of rags over my shoes, so I would be fine for walking in the snow which, when I finally stood up, came all the way to my knees. I began to take some steps toward the area where we had our outhouse. We had no indoor bathroom at that time. The outhouse door was open and there was no life anywhere around it. Our animal sheds were a little way off to the left and I headed toward those. I started to feel uneasy as I heard no sounds from our animals. Normally the pigs would be whining for their dinner and the geese would be hissing for theirs. The chickens would have gone to their nests in the coop.
I heard nothing. But there had been no animal sounds for a long, long time! Slowly, I walked toward the buildings and through my squinting eyelids I saw that all the doors and gates were wide open! There were no animals around, not one. I started to get worried and my fear rose again. It was getting dark and I made no discovery yet. Then, I looked beyond the pigs' pen and saw one of them lying in the snow,

red blood tinting its whiteness. I noticed a few big holes in its head. Then another pig, another, another...all lying in the snow, shot and dead. There were footprints in the snow. Big, deep footprints. I tracked over to one of the pigs and with a trembling little finger, I touched it. It was cold. I counted five of our eight pigs shot down in the snow. I didn't see the other three. There were no geese or chickens, even our dog was gone. I began to cry and I remembered my mother's warning: 'no matter what happens out there, do not make a sound!' I kept on crying silently, inward to myself, just as I cried after each one of my beatings. Silently, inwardly to myself. I was filled with sorrow and I felt lost. I didn't hear when someone walked up to me. I only felt the strong grip on my arm. I jumped and turned and in pure terror saw a man I had never seen before! He was wearing a dark green uniform and boots that reached up to his knees. He wore a hat trimmed in fur, the kind I have not seen before, either. I started to pull away but he grabbed harder onto my arm and yanked on it, so I fell down into the snow. He had an ugly half smile on his face and smelled of strong, stinky tobacco. He had a thick, light colored mustache and his eyes were blue. He said something in a hissing kind of way which, if possible, terrified me even more. With his next move, he had me off the ground and under his arm. I was silent, but I remembered kicking him and I tried to bite his hand. He got angry and said some words I could not understand. He hit me on my head which caused the kerchief that belonged to my grandma, to fall off my head and onto the ground. It was freezing cold. He then threw me onto that kerchief, on the snow and pinned me to the ground. He dug one of his knees into the pit of my stomach, grabbed my hair with one hand and plastered his mouth onto mine. I bit him and he hit me again. I tasted blood. I wasn't sure if it was his or mine. Once he started to unbutton his fly, I already knew what to expect. I wanted to vomit, but did not. Suddenly, my body went still and limp. 'He can't hurt me anymore, no one can hurt me anymore...' were my thoughts.

The taperecorder kept on talking. The next thing I remembered was my grandfather's voice and a slight sensation of cloth touching my skin as he was trying to cover me up. It was dark now and the sun set beyond the rolling hills. My grandfather carefully pulled me up, so I could sit. It was then, that I saw the new red snow, tinted by my own blood. He picked me up into his arms and quietly, but firmly said: *"you will never say a word to anyone about this. If you do, you'll see that no one will ever love you again."*

As if someone did love me now!! I remembered those words from years back. The same warnings. The same pain. Who said those words?

"Just forget it, as if *nothing ever happened*," grandpa added. I looked back to the dead animals. There was one pig missing from the pile of corpses.

'Yeah, a pig needs a pig' I thought still without emotion,' I pig needs a pig.' My grandfather carried me to the cellar door and carefully put me down. The door was open and he gave me a nudge to go inside. I couldn't move. He left me there and went to empty out the container that we used for our body wastes. When he returned I was still standing, motionless, numb. Grandpa locked and bolted the door behind us and together, in the pitch dark, we descended to the belly of the freezing cold cellar. I smelt the familiar sweetness of my grandmother's lavender as I sat on the floor next to her. She took my hand in one of hers and with her other hand she traced my legs under my skirt. She then pulled me onto her lap and cradled me. She began to gently rock the both of us. I had no feelings, no emotions and only one thought: 'I didn't make a sound. I was a good girl." I pulled myself into a ball and with my mind blank I fell into a frozen oblivion. The last thing I remembered was when grandpa handed me a large tin can filled with wine. I bottomed it. My mother did not come near me.

For decades to come, I had nightmares about that evening but could never remember any details until I recalled the true incident under hypnosis. For decades, I was not able to tell a single person about that experience, though I would wake up from a nightmare, drenched in sweat, terrified, never making a sound. My torment did not disturb or frighten anyone else. The last tape clicked off.

I was born under a communist government, so we did not have God. It was forbidden for us children to even think about such a thing! Older people secretly spoke of and about God, but it was for older people to do! They were old, they didn't know any better! We were taught that what you see is and that's all there is. Make it and you'll have it. What little spiritual guidance I received came from my grandmother. This woman was a very petite lady, not even five feet tall. She gave birth to fourteen children and as small as she was, to me she was a giant. A gentle giant! In times of pain and desperation, my thoughts or prayers had been directed toward my grandma. In a curious kind of way, to a little, battered child, she was the only reachable God. Later in my life I knew she understood me and loved me for precisely the child I was. In my early years I went everywhere with her in her daily activities. She taught me about growing things in the garden for food and flavoring. She taught me about herbs for healing, and people would see us, holding hands, often walking in the fields or in the woods, gathering leaves, buds and roots, weeds and mushrooms and other wild - growing vegetation. She would explain to me which was which and how to dry and preserve them, how to combine and use them together for different healing of ailments. Many times she would be quiet and we just walked, hand in hand, my grandma and I.

She talked to me about God at times, too. God became a bonding secret between us. A secret among many other secrets of mine that we never talked about. She explained to me that God is in heaven and if I was good, I would go to heaven one day and I would meet God. I had no idea what was good or bad, so I left the matter alone. The way she described God, he was way out there, far, far away, out of my reach, anyway. I needed someone, anyone to be with me, now! So, she gave me angels to watch over me! I could talk to angels, walk with angels, play with angels. Angels were everywhere and everyone had one, we just couldn't see them.

"What use are they, then?" I asked her.

"Angels come into your life when you believe in them," said my grandma. I guess I believed in them because I often had dreams of being with angels. I remembered very clearly about these dreams and told her about them. One of these dreams became a recurring one for many years, even into my adulthood. In this dream I was a child about three or four years old, wearing a long white gown. I had no wings, but I could push myself up and I would float way above the trees and the house of my grandparents. I would be joyful and I would laugh as I did my swirling, twirling and somersaulting. It was always happening above my grandparents' home. When I woke up in those mornings, I was very happy and filled with wonder. My grandma would say:

"Did you do your angel dance last night?" and she'd smile lovingly at me. Yes, she knew me.

Something kept me in semi-sanity. I was a very smart child, though a loner. I had no friends or children my age around our home to play with. In school I was in classrooms with much older kids, so socially I did not fit in. While girls my age played with dolls, I was studying science. They had pretty dresses and pony-tails I had a short haircut and wore a skirt and white blouse. I did go to ballet classes which I enjoyed a lot. I liked moving my body and I was a pretty good little dancer. Piano lessons did not go well, though. I studied for two years, sitting front of the black and white keyboard, still, reading music did not make any sense to me, when I could read books.

I had a beautiful singing voice, but never really did anything with that either, because I could not learn to read those little balls and sticks among the black lines. Books became my only friends and I collected them. To this day, I love to have books around me, though nowadays I have very little time to read them.

I developed an intense curiosity toward the mind. started to read a lot of philosophy. By the age of ten I was pretty close to Aristotle. Naturally, my loneliness increased, so I read even more. My grandma no longer understood me and I lost contact even with her and her version of God as well.

It would take much too long to detail, what life was like under Russian Regime, after the invasion. Young or old, we all had a devastating life filled with fear, one cannot imagine. I cannot write about it in detail in this book, because to most, my words would be unbelievable. It is enough to say that poverty, hunger, long bread lines with no more bread left at the end of the line was a daily experience. Winters without any type of fuel, not enough warm clothing and the constant presence of hunger occupied our minds and tortured our bodies. If those tortures were not enough, the Russians provided plenty extras to keep a gray gloom of fear and sadness over our heads - all in the name of freedom! Beatings and physical tortures touched nearly every family and even in school the teachers had a free hand at administering severe physical and mental punishments. We new no joy or laughter, only sadness, depression, hunger and pain.

My own emotions developed, nightmares haunted, feelings cried out to be heard. All of them inside of a ten year old, used and abused little girl. All I had was my books and my wine. Hopes, desires or dreams never entered my mind.

My relationship with my parents was very sad and cold. I remember them having lots of fights, whenever I was around. My father openly disliked me, even to a point of saying how much he hated me. One thing stood clear in my mind, which he repeated to me most of my young life:

"You will never amount to anything!"
Oh, one more thing:

"Don't ever have your portrait done, because with a nose as big as yours, you'd need two frames to put around your face."

He took my little brother everywhere with him and continued to administer his routine beatings to my naked little behind. By this time my mother tried to defend me, without success. She would soothe both me and herself with some wine after each of my father's outbursts. I wouldn't even have to ask for it. She just brought it to me and waited a little while until I got numb. We both got numb. That was my life. By that time I hated my father and often wished that he would die. Still, I tried to please him every which way I could, whenever I had the opportunity to do so. Nothing I could do was ever enough or good enough for him. I studied harder and harder. My grades were out of reach. At eleven years of age I chose to study psychology along with philosophy. My teachers were all proud of me. It didn't make me happy. It didn't make him happy, either. Looking back, now with a healthy mind, I see it clearly - the better I tried to be, the more uncomfortable and inadequate he became, the more he needed to pound on me.

I never developed any jealousy toward my bother, even though my family had showered him with more caring, nurturing and affection in one day than I had received in a year! In a lifetime! I truly and deeply loved my brother and still do. Next to my grandma, he had been the only person whom I loved unconditionally, until recent years. He was a sweet and joyful little boy with blonde, almost white hair and beautiful sky blue eyes. I felt a deep love coming from him toward everyone, including myself. He was my little friend. He held my only string of love toward a male human being for most of my life.

After therapy I lost my hair and took to wearing wigs.
Kelly was four years old.

Chapter 7

Bigger Isn't Better

At the age of twelve, I finished high school. I was selected to write the valedictorian address. I was the only one who didn't cry at the reading. The average student's age around me was eighteen.

My father gave a party in my 'honor' at a local restaurant. There were many people there, mostly his friends and I did not know them. There was a lot of drinking and dancing and having a good, noisy time. There were gypsy musicians playing their violins, pouching their tips. It was the first time in my life ever, when I had seen a group of people let loose under the presence of drinking too much. I never let loose. I would just get drunk and fall asleep or pass out, whichever came first. I drank to dull my pain before it got me!

Anyway, I was dancing with these people, from one hand to another, being passed around like some doll. When my father came to dance with me I was already tired and had my own share of drinks. So did he! As he put his hand on my waist I pulled myself away a little and he noticed it. Instead of letting me move back, he pulled me closer to himself with force and I felt his stiffened erection through the folds of my skirt. I became angry and from out of nowhere, I raised my right knee and gave the strongest push I could, upward. In an instant, he was lying on the floor in front of my feet, curled up in a ball, both his hands between his thighs. I looked at him with hate and pity. Then I felt sorry for him. When I looked up, there were many people standing around, looking at both of us.

"Daddy had too much to drink" I said and walked away from them. I went straight to my mother and said to her:

"Keep him away from me and don't ever ask me about this day, Mother!"
My father never once touched, hit or beat me after that day. We spoke very little to one another within the whole family. Soon, I went away to college. I was twelve and a half years old.

As an adult, today I find it difficult to imagine another child with my experiences. Certainly, there are children all over the world suffering some form of abuse, poverty, and famine. I am not implying that I had been the most unfortunate youngster in humanity. Not at all. In many ways I had been very fortunate. I had a home, food, clothing and definitely every opportunity for education and intellectual growth. Had I known to be satisfied with my present moments, I would also have found love. But I wanted love to come from those I expected it to come from and did not receive it. So, I convinced myself to be an unloved child. My grandma's and brother's affections did not quite fill my wants.

I was a very pretty child and grew into a beautiful teenager - I often heard people say. None of that really matters much when you don't have any self-esteem, rather, the self-esteem you do have is so low, it can't sink any lower. When you are not shown or taught respect, you have none. Including self - respect.

I would like so much to paint a picture of a beautiful, smart, well-adjusted child! Instead, I can scribble a sad image of a beautiful, smart, angry and hateful twelve year old alcoholic - lonely, friendless, unloved. I cried myself to sleep most nights, holding my sobs inward, my arms wrapped tightly across my knees as I pulled myself into a tight ball. No one knew what emotions I felt. Not even I. Whatever names they hid behind, they had power over me and kept me their prisoner. I had no friends. The closest

I came to girls my age was, when I watched them from a distance as they played among each other, never asking me to join in their games. From time to time, they would group up and huddle together, sharing some special secret, then look to my direction and snicker, even laugh out loud. Sharing secrets or...I had my own secrets. So many secrets! More than I could remember. I never shared my secrets with anyone!

I continued with ballet lessons. Dancing was my only form of release. I don't know if I was any good or not, I just know how much I enjoyed moving my body.
After dance class I would stay way past lesson time and practice at the bar as I watched my body move in the mirror in front of me.
"She is very graceful," my teacher once said to my mother. Big deal! I would make believe that I was a prima ballerina in one opera or another and I would dance and dance all alone 'til my limbs shook from exhaustion. I'd be so happy! Then, I'd get dressed and grudgingly walk the three miles home. There, I would have my usual wine and crawl to bed, curling up into my little ball and start to cry. That was my childhood.

Our education system was different, from the one we now have here. We went to school from 8:00 AM to 3:00 PM. After that, we had lunch and study hall right there in school. If you were a good student, you had privileges such as ballet or private music and voice classes which you could attend after your homework was done for the following day. A normal school day ended around 6 PM. Our weeks were from Monday through Saturday and we attended school all year round. During the winter we had two weeks of break, one week in late spring and again, in August two more weeks. That's all. The rest of the time: school, study, school, study. No choices.

For a girl like me, it was just fine. I had no other life, so I needed no time for anything else. I would not have known what to do with free time. Yeah, I do: get drunk and curl up into a ball and cry myself to sleep, just as I did for the past twelve years.

Out of high school, into college. I was ready to go back to my studies at the end of August, 1960. No expectations really, just wanting to get away from home. I hated being at home. I lived in fear most of the time, drunk and numb the rest. Very predictable. The fact that I would be around adults now, did not bother me. I was always the youngest, smartest, drunkest, wherever I went. I wondered if they'd let me continue drinking? I was sure of it.

My mother came with me to get me settled in the dorm of the university. We needed very little to bring, since everything was provided by the government. Only personal things.

"Are you going to need anything, dear?" asked my mother.

"Just money. Just spending money." I answered her.

"What do you need that for?" She sounded genuinely surprised. I looked at her:

"I didn't see a big wine barrel anywhere, when they took us on tour, did you? How else do you think I'm going to get my wine, steal it?" I was serious. "Make sure dad sends me enough money to buy my wine. I don't want to run out. You know that it's medicine for me. It helps me to sleep." I was sharp with her.

"Well, we were hoping that you would give it up once you got here," said my mother in a meek little voice.

"What? You were hoping? You, of all people?" I was vicious: "No money, no wine, no school! I'll be back at home and you'll be stuck with me! I'm too young to work, yet. Can you imagine having me at home? Twenty four hours a day? Every day?" It was no beauty speaking. I was screaming at her! Out of nowhere or maybe because I was no longer at home and I didn't have to go back home, an abundant supply of courage surfaced in me. I can't ever remember speaking in that tone of voice to anyone - young or old. We were both surprised. I felt as if I was let out of a cage and about to be put into prison! Prison of sobriety. Except I didn't really consciously know that at the time. I just had a very real reason to panic: no wine!

"I'll talk to your father," said my confused mother.

"You gonna do what? You had better do much better than that! You have to promise me that I will not be out of wine while I am up here! Forget about talking to him! You send me the money! You steal it if you have to but get that money to me! Whatever you have to do, just do it!" (Evil forces defending their sins!)

She promised, just to shut me up. After that scene we had little else to say to each other. We walked around the spectacular, park - like grounds of the dorm, as my mother kept sighing her usual: 'I don't know what to do' sigh. When the taxi came we gave each other a forced hug and off she went. I returned to my room, after having lost myself several times through the various corridors of the dorm.

There were three of us in the same room. I was put with an eighteen and a nineteen year old girl. They were already acquainted with each other, as I walked into the room. You cannot imagine the look on their faces when they saw me! I don't know who was more surprised: the two of them at seeing me or me, seeing the expressions on their faces! The two girls were disgusted at the thought of rooming with a twelve and a half year old, they told me later, after we became close enough for them to consider me a human being. Human being?

They soon learned that we could party with my ever - flowing wine, which they purchased for us with the money my mother managed and never failed to smuggle to me throughout the next five years. I became their confidant and keeper of secrets. They were both pretty girls, very pretty. A little too silly sometimes for my quiet nature, but I learned to laugh from and with them as I listened to one story or another, mostly about boys and our male professors.

Once in a while they secretly brought in a boy or two and I would overhear their giggling and making out in the dark room. I didn't like to eavesdrop, yet once in a while I found myself envious of them. I also discovered a kind of excitement I didn't feel before. As they relived their dates when telling me about the things they did, I began to imagine myself in their places. Part of me wanted to have those experiences and part of me knew what those were, already. Not consciously, but somehow I just knew. I shuddered.

I continued to be a good student, though I was no longer the outstanding best. I had major competition, still, I held my ground. Either this or going back home! Anything, but that!

On my thirteenth birthday my roommates gave me a little party at a local bar. It was the very first time I ever entered a public drinking place. But there was wine, so everything was great. They each had a boyfriend already and the boys came along. The relationship between us three girls grew to be pretty nice. They liked showing off the kid with the brains and the fact that I was also pretty didn't hurt. On some nights, I would dance for them in our room and I even taught them a few ballet poses and positions.

Anyway, on this big day of my thirteenth birthday the five of us were having a real good time. Other kids from campus joined in, some foreign students, too. We had a nice, lively group growing when a boy, whom I had not notice before, joined us. He was the most beautiful boy I had ever seen! Through my hazy gaze I could see how different he was from all the other boys! Tall, slim and dark. He had dark hair and dark eyes. He was dressed exceptionally well, if that meant anything. He had a perfect haircut. And he was quiet. Nice and quiet. Not bored or boring. He spoke to the kids and he smiled, flashing his beautiful, white, even teeth. He was beautiful! Did he know how beautiful he was? Who cares! I knew he was beautiful. And quiet.

When I was introduced to him as the 'star' of the party, he smiled at me, came next to me and gave me a gentle kiss on the cheek.

"I hope it's a nice one," he whispered into my ear. Even his voice was beautiful! I felt a pang, no, more like a big bang in my chest, my heart raced like an airplane engine, I broke into a sweat and I wanted to die! No, I wanted to look into his eyes! No way, I wanted to die! 'What in the world is happening to me? Is this what people called: puppy love?' Well, this puppy came in a size of an English sheep dog, slobbering all over! My head began to throb. Yes, I fell in love on my thirteenth birthday with an older man! He was eighteen!

I fell in love and I fell apart. For days after that evening, I did not see him anywhere on campus. I was too embarrassed to ask either of the girls about him. Since I had no training in emotional development, I had no idea what to do with my feelings. All I knew was, that there were new things developing inside of me fast, things which I could not name, either. I tried to put them in that back room with all the other nameless feelings, but this one did not want to stay there. I kept feeling new things without names and they hurt. Hurt real bad! I had pain in my heart, my stomach, my head and many other places. New places! No one to tell about them, no one to explain them to me, no one to make it better! Not at home, not here. The only friend I had was my alcohol. Within three days, we became very close friends. Real buddies!

I started to miss classes and lectures, for the first time since I began school. My grades were falling and they were falling fast! My pain was unbearable and my alcohol was all that could keep my pain away. There were days when I could not get out of bed. I would fall out, crawl to the bathroom, throw up all over the toilet, the floor, myself and crawl back, only to have another big gulp from the bottle which I kept under my pillow. When I ran out of the wine I drank the brandy the girls bought for me on my birthday.

My roommates became alarmed and went to the dorm's director for help. Our director had to have been the ugliest woman alive! Any person could have nightmares about her! I did. Her name was Olga. Olga was a giant of a woman. She had a deep and mean voice and a grip firm enough to hold up the statue of Atlas! I was genuinely afraid of her. Well, Olga arranged for me to see our campus doctor whom I already had met once, during our physical at admission. He was very handsome and I guess kind of young looking. As far as I could remember, all other doctors I've met before him had been pretty old - but this doctor was not that old.

The following day in fear, shame and pain I got myself as ready as I could. I had to drink myself into some kind of calm state so I could face both questioning and discipline plus whatever imagined horrors might await me. I did not get drunk, but I felt no pain and the alcohol made me mellow and brave and it filled me with false confidence.
I was set to face any problem that day, I thought.

It was late in the afternoon by the time the doctor got around to see me. His office was a typical medical office: smelled like medicine and disinfectants, furnished in government - green metal. No frills. Because we had to put in certain hours of practical studies, the nursing staff was part of the medical branch of the student body. Beside myself, there was one other student waiting, who had a small burn on the top of one of her hands and the student nurse led her into an exam room, at the time motioning me toward the direction, where the doctor was waiting for me.

I knocked, turned white as a ghost and after hearing the doctor's voice, I entered the office. I was scared. The doctor did not look up from his papers, just pointed to a metal chair, one of many, to sit down. I did, gladly. This was the first time in my life that I could remember facing some figure of authority because of my drinking. I knew it had everything to do with my drinking! Even though I drank my way all through schools, somehow no one but no one ever had said anything to me about it. I was a perfect 'A' student, pretty, polite and adorable. All of my teachers and principals seemed to love me and displayed me at times of academic contests, knowing well that I will surpass all the other kids. I didn't let them down. There was no reason to rock the boat, so as long as I did well and caused no disturbance, they left me alone in my need. That is just the way things were there and then!

I feared discipline and in my fear, sitting in front of the ugly green metal desk with the doctor behind it, I felt my chest tighten, my fists tighten, my whole body tighten.
I imagined myself getting more beatings, going to jail, sent home and get more beatings from my father! My imagination fed my fear and vice versa. I started to cry as quietly as I could keep, staring at the doctor, waiting for something to happen. When he finally looked up at me, he must have been more puzzled than I was scared, seeing my face and the two rivers of tears pouring from my eyes. His expression was that of total surprise. It did not occur to me that it was my youth which surprised him, not my tears. I guess he didn't remember me from the time of registration. He stood up from behind the ugly green desk, walked toward me and sat down on the chair next to me.

"How old are you?" he asked.

"Thirteen. I just had a birthday." I whispered to him, looking at my hands as I clutched them together in my lap, knuckles white.

"Who sent you here?" He asked again.

"The director of the dorm. Maybe I'm not supposed to be here!" I was ready to get up and run out of there.

"Yes you are," said the doctor. "Tell me, why are you crying?"

"Because I am afraid of you...I know I'm in trouble and I don't want to get a beating. I don't want to get dismissed and sent home! I don't want to go home!"
I looked up at him, pleading.

"I'm not sending you home. Here, wipe your eyes and nose. Calm down. I'm not going to beat you, either." He gave me his handkerchief and I obeyed, blowing my nose into it.

"That's *a good girl*. Now, how about a smile? There. You are very, very pretty. I bet lots of people tell you that." He was friendlier than I ever dreamed a doctor could be. Men in my family didn't talk to me like that. Nice doctor!

"Now, will you tell me why your director sent you here?"

"Because I have been sick. I have been staying in bed for days. Almost a week now." I was dodging.

"Are you hurt?"

"Yes."

"Where do you hurt?"

"Everywhere, mostly inside at places I can't name." With wet eyes I looked up at him, again. He smiled.

"Can you put your finger to it?"

"No! It's not on my body. This pain is coming from someplace inside!"

"What does it feel like?" asked the doctor.

"It feels like it's choking me. My heart feels like something is squeezing it tight. Sometimes I get dizzy.
I cry."

"How often do you feel that way?"

"Always. Day and night. It's real bad lately."
I started to open up to a total stranger. A doctor. A man!

"Anything new happened lately?" he asked.

84

"Yes. I met a boy." That was all I said. I looked at him as if I just revealed the greatest secret in the whole world. I did!

"Yes?" He was puzzled. At age thirteen meeting a boy and getting infatuated was a normal event of growing into adulthood. Not for me, but he didn't know that.

"Have you been taking anything for your pain?"

"Yes. Wine and brandy." I said without hesitation.

"Oh? How much?"

"Well...it's like...I don't know. Until the pain stops." I honestly didn't think about how much alcohol I consumed.

"When does the pain stop?"

"As I'm falling asleep."

"How often do you need to drink?" he asked curiously.

"Every day."

"Every day? How long have you been needing to drink?" He was very curious.

"Oh...well...I guess a long time now. I guess as long as I can remember." I still didn't think there was anything unusual about that. Most especially, since kids at the dorm also drank. I had even seen our dorm director drunk, on more than a few occasions. (The fact, that earlier I was sure that my being drunk had been the very reason for that visit no longer existed. I was not hurting right then, so I bravely defended my drinking problem.)

"So, you have been drinking for a long time. Right?"

"Yes...well guess so. I guess I always have. When I don't drink, I get very sick. After I have some wine, the pain inside starts to go away and then I fall asleep." What was the big deal about that, anyway! Everybody drinks. What's so unusual about that! I was feeling no pain and getting upset with him. He noticed the shift in my mood.

"Tell me about this boy." He changed the topic.
'How can I,' I thought 'I don't know anything about him!' I looked into the doctor's eyes. They were warm and he looked really interested. He was smiling at me.

"It's all right, I am not going to tell anyone about it. I'm a doctor, you know that I have to keep everything a secret." He assured me.

"You have secrets, too?" I asked him.

"Hundreds of them. Do you?"

"Oh, yes, but not hundreds, only a few. I'm not supposed to tell anyone, though. A lot of my secrets I can't even remember anymore. I just know that I have them." He took my hands into his and held them firmly. His were nice and warm and dry. Mine were tiny, cold and clammy but he showed no sign of noticing it.

"You can tell me everything you want to, if it will make you feel better." I believed him and I started to cry again, quietly. He pulled my head on his chest and patted my hair, gently. I began to talk. At first it was just a jibber, not making much sense, but I worked it into a full blown confession, all the way back to the time when I remembered receiving my first beating from my daddy. Yet, when he asked me, I couldn't remember why my father gave me that terrible beating. Mostly, I could not remember any causes, only fears, tears and a terrible ache inside of me.

The doctor gave me some pills to take to calm me down and made another appointment for the following week. He gave me very strict instructions not to take any alcohol with my pills and made me promise that I will return to my lectures the following morning. I did both. I liked this doctor a lot, though he really did not do anything other than listen to me. Finally, for the first time in my life, someone was interested in hearing what I was feeling, what I had to say. He didn't hit me or beat me for the things I had done, nor did he ever say that I was a bad girl. He didn't really say much at all. He just listened. No one, as far as I could remember had ever listened to what I had to say. Truthfully, I never even dared to say anything to anyone, until now. But this was a doctor and he was a keeper of hundreds of secrets, after all! It was O.K. My only wish was that I could have remembered more to tell him. But each time I started to relate something to him, I would have no actual memory of the causes. I became frustrated with myself. Deep down in my heart I really wanted to confess to him. But what?

I did feel a little better through the days to come. I found myself eager to see the doctor again. The pills that he gave me were tranquilizers. Very powerful tranquilizers, I found out much later, to which I became very heavily addicted during the almost five years of my college time. He provided them for me at my demand and had them readily available, even after my graduation. In fact, I brought with me enough to last throughout an entire year, when I defected to the US.

I had also graduated from a small town wino to a big city junky. For entertainment I learned to use the two combined together.

Bigger Isn't Better.

By early 1972 my hair grew enough to let go of the wigs.
Carla kept me serene and at peace.

Chapter 8

The Beauty and The Beast

As a good girl, I kept my appointment with the doctor and was very expectant to see him. I held up my end of our bargain: did not drink any alcohol, returned to my classes and lectures and even though I was still far behind in making up the missed hours, I did have a couple of good reports to relate to him.

I had, on few occasions, also seen Laci, the boy of my heartache, on campus. I was thrilled when he had waved to me in recognition. We had some lectures scheduled together, but our auditoriums were too huge to expect to meet in one. I had a very difficult time concentrating on my work, forever thinking about his beautiful face. I was ready to talk to my doctor about that, too.

My second appointment with the doctor was on the last day of November 1960, a very cold winter day already. I wanted to make a really good impression, so I decided to dress up real pretty. Wearing a straight black, pipe skirt with a thick, pale pink wool sweater and little black pumps. I really looked like an adorable dancer with a perfect little body. As I looked at myself in the mirror of our bathroom, I realized that my body was older than the rest of me. Already developed and shapely, I didn't look like a simple, scared thirteen year old.

"Look at you," said one of my roommates." You look grown up enough to make any older man fall for you! You are beautiful!" She chirped on as I blushed and enjoyed the compliment.

"I think it's those pills, the doctor gave me. I kind of feel older, just a little."

"Well, Baba, you will turn a few heads on campus today, it's for sure. I have to look out for the new competition!" she teased.

"Don't worry. You think I should change?" I didn't want to be competition.

"Only for today, you can stay as you are. But only for today!" she laughed at my discomfort. "Wait until Laci sees you dressed like this. He'll really flip!" Agi was the teaser and Eva was the flirt.

The three of us rode the electric car to the university every day, since my visit to the doctor. My two roommates took to caring for me and about me, though we didn't ever talk about my drunkenness the weeks before. Denial.

My first class was at 7:30 AM, biology. Laci also had that same class. My eyes automatically searched the huge auditorium to find him. They did! I know I blushed when his hand went up to wave to me. But, instead of waving back, I looked beyond him as if I didn't notice him. I don't know why, I just did. Kid's stuff. I felt people's, well, men's eyes on me, staring at me. I don't know if anyone really was looking at me or I just imagined it because of what Agi had said earlier. I sat down. Feeling my heart race again, I reached for the bottle and took a small blue pill the doctor gave me. I could take one every four hours if I needed one. I needed one right then.

"You are really beautiful today" a voice whispered in my ear and the warm breath sent shivers down my neck and back. 'Laci!' I thought and jumped up, a little startled. He was standing, bent over, one row behind me. I didn't even see him approach, nor did I pay attention to any movements around me. I was busy with my little blue pills.

"Anyone sitting next to you?" asked Laci in that beautiful voice of his.

"I think so," said I.

"Well, not for long. We are just switched." And with that, he stepped over the back of the seat and slipped into it.

"You know, I have been tying to get close to you since the evening of your birthday.   Your roommates were supposed to help me out, but I heard you got very sick soon after that evening. I wanted to come and see you but they said it's best I stayed away. Are you O.K. now? You sure look stunning!" he kept on talking in his beautiful, quiet voice.

"Yes, I am much better now. I have a lot of work to make up. I fell far behind, so I've been studying very hard to catch up." I was nervous.

"I'd like to help, if you let me. I'm not very smart or anything like that, but if I can help, you know I'd like to. Are you sure you're only thirteen? It's hard to believe. You make me a little nervous."

"Yeah, I'm just a kid. You don't have to study with me. I'll be just fine." The pill didn't help. My heart was racing still and I felt a kind of disappointment, which I didn't understand. Clothes or no clothes, I was just a kid.

"But I want to, I really do," insisted Laci.

The professor walked into the huge room and the student body turned silent. I took my notebook and pen and readied myself for an hour and a half filled with bacteria and viruses, courtesy of a British professor. Laci set next to me, creating his own notes. We were quiet and completely absorbed in our purpose. Higher education.
I did not think of him being in the seat next to me for the entire hour and a half. When the professor finished, we all applauded in recognition of his knowledge. I looked over at Laci and said to him:

"I am going to have to change teachers."

"Why?" his dark eyes stared at me.

"I have a very difficult time understanding his accent. I'm too far behind already to have to struggle this hard."

"I'll help you. I really want to help you."

"I don't know. College is really hard for me. I used to just fly through my classes. But now? Now I struggle so hard. I'm not the whiz - kid anymore. I don't know. I'll have to talk to my doctor about it."

"What time is your lunch break today" asked Laci.

"I don't know. At one, I guess? I'm not sure. I have some anatomy lessons to make up and I'm still short of a paper that was long do. I'm going to study during lunch break." Laci was sweet, attentive and I began to feel uncomfortable. Too much attention, I suppose. I wasn't used to attention. Not this kind.

"Well, I'm free at one also, so why don't you let me study with you?"

"C'mon, you don't have to do that. I told you, I'm just a kid and you are already grown up! You're eighteen years old! We got hundreds of girls your age at this university. You don't want to be with me." I couldn't believe I was actually saying those words!

"Hello, Laci, ready for chemistry?" A beautiful blonde came up to us and she slipped her arm through his.

"Yeah, sure," he said, smiling at the gorgeous girl. As they were walking away, Laci looked back and shouted: "At one! I'll be there," and he winked at me. I kept looking at them for a while. My heart never had a chance to slow down and it was back on a faster track. Why? I felt what one might call jealous. But why? Well, he was with a gorgeous blonde, that's why! But when he was with me, I didn't feel good, either. I didn't want him so near me. Why? What is going on with me! 'Well, I sure hope the doctor has a lot of time for me today,' I thought. I took another little blue pill.

One o'clock came too fast and too slow, both at the same time. What is going on with me today! Laci was at the dining room door, lazily leaning against the frame, looking down at the floor, his hands hidden in the depth in his pockets. I stopped in my tracks, not believing that he actually kept his word. When I stood in front of him, he didn't look up. He just took a deep breath, removed his hands from his pockets and took my books.

"I didn't think you'd come." He said and then he looked up and smiled, showing off those whiter than white perfect teeth of his.

"I really want to study with you." He added.

"I believe you. Well, I'm trying to, anyway. It's just that I have never been with anyone who is as nice to me as you are. I guess I'm afraid or something." I was afraid and it was something. But what?

"We better eat and get to work, if you're gonna believe in me!" He gave me a gentle push across my back. We ate in silence, as I kept thinking of the gorgeous blonde from earlier in the day. I decided to ask him about her.

"Who is the blonde?"

"Huh?" Laci looked up from his plate.

"The blonde, this morning. Who is she?"

"She's a beautiful girl who thinks she can get everything and everyone with her looks."

"Can she?"

"She thinks she can."

"Can she?"

"No."

Anatomy was not the subject to begin studying together. It had a totally new meaning and I did not get my work done. Laci knew it, too.

"We'll work around it, O.K.? Baba, I'd really like to spend some time with you. I know I'm much older than you are, but it's not my fault. There is no one here your age and even if there were any boys as young as you, would you really have anything in common with them? All I am trying to do is get to know you. Don't worry about the blonde. I'm not going to hurt you." He spoke very quietly, as before. I thought: 'I am already hurting, I just don't know why.'

"I'll have to see the doctor today." I said to him.

"What does that have to do with anything?"

"I don't know. I just...I don't know."

"Do you want me to go with you to his office? Are you afraid of him?"

"Oh, no! At first I was afraid, but not anymore. He's very nice. Very nice."

"Can I wait for you after your visit?"

"It's not necessary. I'll see you tomorrow. I'm starting at eight but I'll be in the library by seven. You know, I have a lot..."

"...of making up to do. Yes, I know. I'll be there. I'll help you if I can." Laci seemed disappointed. I didn't understand what was going on.

The entire day was confusing. I didn't get much work done and I felt under pressure. I believed his offer of help but I didn't feel secure about it. Why would a man like Laci want to spend any time with a kid like me? I could hardly wait for my doctor's appointment.

As before, I was the last patient. His office door was wide open and when he heard the door close, he called out my name. I walked into his office. He smiled at me and walked out from behind his ugly green desk.

"Hello there, beautiful girl> How are you feeling?" The doctor asked in a very friendly voice.

"O.K., I guess."

"I saw you on campus today. More than once, as a matter of fact! Every male turned to look at you, twice!"

"Sure." Just what I needed to hear.

"You don't believe me?"

"Oh, I don't know, I guess. I don't feel much like a grown up. I feel more like a very scared kid." I was telling him the truth.

"Why?" asked the doctor.

"I just do. The more attention I got today, the more scared I felt. Like if something bad is gonna happen. Even my roommates made me nervous."

"Want to tell me about it?" He came close, sat down on one of the ugly green metal chairs, gently pulling me to sit next to him. He had taken my left hand into his and was now petting it, reassuring me.

"I spent a lot of time with the boy that I met on my birthday. Today, he came to sit next to me...and we had lunch together...and tomorrow I'm meeting him again at the library..." I detailed my day to him.

"I wasn't so much afraid as...I just didn't know what to say or what to do. I'm not used to people being nice to me. When they are, I don't know why they are nice. I don't know what they want from me. I don't know what to say to them. I don't know what to do! So, I just feel really stupid and very uncomfortable. It scares me when people are nice. I just don't know anything!"

"Do I scare you, too?" the doctor asked.

"A little."

"Do you think I want to hurt you?"

"Oh, no. Do you?"

"No. You are very young and very inexperienced. Naturally, you would be scared. I was scared at your age, too!"

"You were?"

"Sure. You are a very beautiful, young girl. Do you think that you are beautiful?"

"No. I don't think about myself that way. I just think how out of place I am. No matter where I go, I am out of place. Too young, too old, too smart, too pretty, too something! Never just right. Never."

"Don't worry about it. You'll grow into the right places and then you will fit into everywhere. You have to learn to see yourself differently from now on. You know that you are smart, right?"

"I guess, or else I would still be in high school."
I laughed a little.

"That's right. You are smart, intelligent and beautiful. Even your hands are beautiful. Did you ever look at your hands? See? Perfect little hands, long, slender, tapered fingers. Pretty pink skin, not a single mark on it. Stand up. See? You are slim and rather tall for your age. You have long, strong legs, a thin body and nice, slim arms. You have a long neck, beautiful reddish hair, sparkling green eyes and tiny ears. Your lips are nice and perky and..."

"...and my nose is big enough to need two frames!" I broke into a cry, my tears running down my cheeks.

"You have a nice nose! Where did you ever hear such foolishness?"

"My father told me."

"Does your father have a big nose?"

"Kind of," I said after thinking for a second.

"Well, he can keep it! Your nose is very nice. Not too big, not to small."

" Then what is wrong with me? Why do I always feel so bad?" I was crying again. He kept silent.

"You know, I didn't drink any wine, just like you told me last week. I have been taking the little blue pills, like you told me to. But when I forget to take it, I start feeling really bad all over again. What is wrong with me, Doctor?" I cried and didn't feel very pretty.

"You are growing up and no one told you that growing up means changing. Your body is changing and so are your feelings. You will notice lots of changes in your body as you become a woman."

"I already have breasts! I already am a woman! My dance teacher told me about those things when I was eleven years old. I have been a woman for two years and I still don't feel good!" I continued to cry.

"When was the last time a doctor examined you?"

"Did what?"

"Your last examination. What is the doctor's name?"

"I don't have a doctor. I once had a high fever and an old doctor came to our house. He took my temperature and gave me a shot. I almost died after the shot. I'm not supposed to take penicillin, because I have an allergy. I was seven years old, then. When I was ten, I had a very bad earache. That doctor gave me some powder to take. He was very old, too. That's all. You are the third doctor I had to see and you gave me pills to take."

"Well, I have to examine you, then." He stood up and took me by my left arm, leading me into another room.

96

"Take your clothes off."

"Do what? Why?"

"So I can examine you. I can't do it with your clothes on."

"I don't want to take my clothes off! What will you do to me?" My eyes were wide open and I no longer trusted him.

"I have to listen to your heart, your lungs, your stomach and so on. I can't do it with all those clothes on! I know you're scared, but you don't need to be. Relax. Take this little blue pill and everything will be calmer."

"It doesn't help. Most of the time the pill doesn't help much. Most of the time I've been taking two little pills."

"Then take two of them. Here." He handed me two of the little blue pills and a glass with some water in it.

"I wish it was wine," I looked up and said to him.

"Maybe later. Now, just sit up on this table and take off your clothes. I'll be right back. If you want to, you can lay down." He left the room and I relaxed a little.

I kept sitting on the table and all of a sudden I started to feel very warm. Very warm! Warm and kind of light headed. Relaxed. My fingertips started to tingle and my arms felt heavy. I just continued sitting on that table feeling very relaxed, warm and numb by the time the doctor returned. And dizzy. Relaxed, numb and dizzy.

"How are you doing? I see you still have your clothes on."

"I feel numb all over. I feel like I'm going to fall off! I need help."

"Let me help you. Pull your arm out, now the other. Good. Now, over the head. *Good girl.*" I saw him staring at my breasts. I was not wearing a bra. We did not wear bras in those days at the age of thirteen.

"Oh my, you are more beautiful than I had imagined! You are truly beautiful." He whispered.

"You had been imagining me...." My words slurred.

"Every day..." He pulled off both my little black pumps and knee highs, then the waist of my skirt. He laid me flat on my back and pulled my skirt down and off of my legs.

"I have never seen anything so beautiful in my life. You are beautiful!" He took his stethoscope and placed it on my chest.

"Take a deep breath, Baba." I breathed. I saw my naked breasts dart up in the air, then fall. I could not keep my eyes open. I felt groggy. He kept moving the cold piece of metal all over my chest, my breasts, my stomach, my abdomen, all the while saying how beautiful I was. Then, I could no longer feel the metal, only his hands. I felt him kiss my hair as he was caressing my face, my neck, my ears, tracing the outline of my lips and touching them with his. I could not believe what was happening! I couldn't move nor make a sound. I couldn't open my eyes. I didn't want to open my eyes! My doctor was touching me all over! He fondled my breasts and I felt my thighs gently pulled apart, my waist lifted up and my panties being pulled down over my legs, my knees, my feet.

I felt many other things, even pain, but more from a distance as if I was no longer there, though I knew that I was.

"You little bitch!" He finally changed his tone. "And I thought you were innocent, all along!" There was a painful thrust at my lower body and then I passed out.

The room was dark when I came to. Some kind of cover was draped over my body. I felt alone. I listened in a half stupor for sounds, any sound at all. Dead silence.

"Is anybody there?" I whispered.

"I'm here." Answered the doctor.

"Why did you hurt me...? The doctor was sitting on a chair in the dark, some distance from the table I was still lying on. He stood up and came to stand next to me.

"I'm sorry," his voice was a mere whisper. "Who had you been with before?" he asked.

"No one. I have never been with a man before. I have never even kissed a boy before, not even Laci." My silent tears fell to my ears and down to the pillow.

"I'm sorry. I don't know what come over me...you are so very beautiful. Please, believe me. How long have you been dancing?"

"Since I was three years old."

"That must be it, then You must have broken yourself during some dance practice." He was talking to himself.

"Do you still dance, Baba?"

"Only at the dorm. I don't have time anymore. I am far behind in...why did you hurt me?"

"...Yes, of course, I know you told me. What do you want to be when you're done with your studies?" He was upsct and nervous, I thought. I was afraid and I was in pain, I knew. It was a while, before I spoke again:

"*Free. I want to be free.*" I said. Free from what? I had no idea.

"Am I going to have a baby, now?"

"I hope not!" Said the doctor defensively. "Don't worry about that right now." He tried to assure us both quietly, yet agitated.

"I have to get home." I tried to move, but still couldn't . The room, the whole world seemed very distant and even though I was lying steady and motionless, everything around me seemed to move and sway. I was feeling nauseous and had the urge to vomit. My stomach was fast running upstream and suddenly I just bolted upright and threw up all over the doctor.

"Damn, look what you did!" he yelled and looked at himself in disgust.

"I threw up all over you" I answered calmly, expecting that he will slap me across my face. He did not.

"I have to go to the bathroom." I said to him. I had another wave of nausea rushing in my stomach. Too late, this time I vomited all over the floor. I heaved and heaved, my tears pouring down my face. I didn't care. Some feelings began to return to my body and I held fast onto the table's edge I was sitting on. The room was spinning around me. I felt like I was going to pass out again. All I could remember was some hands grabbing onto my arms as I was about to fall off of the table, right into my vomit. Then, the world went black again.

"I want to die." I heard my own voice saying when I finally came to. I smelt something strong and very awful and there was a cloth at my mouth. The doctor got some chemical for me to inhale and bring me about.

"I can't believe this!" I heard him say. "You can't tell about this to anybody, you understand? If you do, surely, the dean will dismiss you right away and you get sent back home! Nobody is going to believe you, anyway! It wasn't even my fault, damn it!" He carried on.

'Of course not, it's all mine. Everything is always my fault,' I thought to myself. Besides, who am I going to tell, anyway? I would be sent home. He's right. No one would believe a thirteen year old kid, anyway? So, what's to tell!? All of a sudden I felt alone and abandoned again.

"I will never again trust another man for as long as I live! You out there, all of you, you're gonna pay for this!" I was filled with hate and a burst of energy.

"I have to go home!" I said with such coldness, my own voice shocked me. "Don't bother helping me, I'll get myself out of here. I'm not going to clean up." I was filled with anger and hate, despair and fear and I could have killed him in my mind.

"I was going to escort you, but now I smell so awful, I can't!" He complained.

"Escort me? But of course!" I replied curtly. "Don't bother, I don't need an escort. I've been through worse than this. At the back of my mind I knew I spoke the truth, but I couldn't remember what truth it was.

I got dressed and left the office, the building, the campus grounds. It was dark and cold. Thoughtlessly, with a blank mind, I followed my little feet to the street car to take me home. Once I was safe inside the dorm, I showered as fast as I could and went straight to bed. I curled up into my little ball and wished for someone to hold me, love me, comfort me. I was so alone, so afraid, so broken, I couldn't even think. I knew that I didn't want to get sent home to my parents' house. Never again! Never!

'I hate every man, every boy in the whole world! Even the ones that haven't been born yet!' And I did.

I woke up to muffled sounds of scuffle. It was still dark outside our window, but my two roommates were awake, getting ready for school. I had to get up! I felt heavy and lifeless. 'No, you can't do this. Don't think about yesterday afternoon. You can't stay here! You have lots of work to do, yet. Nothing happened. I hate men! All of them. Well, maybe not Laci. Maybe him, too!' I kept having my own dialogue. I got out of bed and dragged myself through the morning routine.

"Library, 7:00 AM. I'll be there." Laci's voice echoed in my mind.

'But that was yesterday, today I hate men.'
I answered myself. 'Nothing happened. You have to make believe that nothing happened. He'll notice a change otherwise! You want him to know? Of course not. Nothing happened, so there is no reason for you not to be on time. Go on, nothing happened! Nothing!'

Laci was waiting for me at the entrance of the library. Just as I approached him, a student walked over to me and handed me a slip of paper.

"Report to doctor's office at 7:50 AM," said the note.

"Thank you" I told the girl and stuffed the paper into my coat pocket.

"Early morning love letter?" smiled Laci with a curious look on his face.

"Doctor's note." I said and showed him the small piece of paper. He relaxed. We studied silently and I got up from the table at 7:45 AM, sharp.

"I'll see you later. Thank you for your time."

"I'll go with you!" He closed his book and stood up himself.

"No. Maybe some other time" I forced a smile. I was thankful for not having to say anything during the last three quarters of an hour.

"I just wanted to see how you are doing, how you are feeling this morning," said the doctor smiling.

"You should know, you are the doctor. Do you want to examine me again?" I lashed out at him. I think he expected me to be more timid. I know, I did. But no, not me! The same feeling came over me, as did at the time of my graduation party, after I danced with my father. Hate.

"You don't have to be so nasty," said the doctor, much more quietly, *"nothing happened."*

"If nothing happened, then why am I here?"

"Well, last night you didn't take your supply of pills. Here. Here they are." He handed me a larger bottle than the one I had before. I unscrewed the cap, and there they were. My baby blues. I took one, then another, right in front of him.

"Anything else?" I asked.

"I'll be calling you and checking on you."

"Fine, just don't call me to talk, again." I hated him!

"And don't send me to another doctor to talk, either! I 'talked' enough! I'll never talk to a doctor about myself either. I'll never talk to men, again! I hate you, all!" I was aching inside and wished I could cry. But I couldn't. So, I just clenched my fists at my sides and bit down on my teeth. Just as I did each time my father was beating me.

"I'll let you know when I'm out of pills." I walked out of the office. I expected, that he would call after me, get me to return and discipline me. It didn't happen.

My life changed once again, for the worse. The result of that last evening of November 1960 both ended and began on August 28, 1961, when I gave birth to a tiny, seemingly healthy little boy named Robert. I was thirteen and a half years old. The birth was early and easy, the pregnancy was not. Shortly after winter break, I got called into the doctor's office again.

"How are you feeling?"

"Why do you want to know?" I retorted.

"Because I do. Had you notice any changes in your body, since I saw you last?"

"With or without my clothes on?" I was nasty and fearless.

"The last time." He spoke quietly.

"My breasts hurt and they grew." I told him. "Now, can I go?"

"No. What do you mean 'they grew'? How do they hurt?" He seemed concerned.

"I mean they are sore. Very sore. But you can't examine me!"

"Fine. If they get worse, come see me." He turned and walked out of his own office, shutting the door behind himself. I returned to my class a few minutes late, missing some of the lecture. I was angry. By then, I learned to take the little blue pills without water. I would imagine that I'm biting into a big yellow lemon and my mouth would fill with saliva and I swallow the little blue pill with it. Simple. It worked every time! I took two.

By the end of January, I began to put on weight. First, I thought it was because I stopped dancing and being as active as I used to be. Laci noticed, also. He and I became friends at best. He was sweet and attentive, the attitude he maintained with me throughout our entire time together. We never even kissed. He would hold me close in his arms from time to time and that was it. I never allowed him any closer. He was a man and as far as I was concerned, he belonged to the category of *men* - sweet or not. And I hated all men.

I did allow the doctor to examine me, after I began to suspect that I had a baby growing inside of me. I was right and he confirmed it. Amazingly enough, I was not panicking. My pregnancy became a matter of fact for me, a condition that would end. I had no emotions about it.
I couldn't feel anything. I was already an emotional cripple, a handicapped soul.

The doctor assured me that he would take care of the baby, when the time came. He and his wife will keep it. He would even put her name on the birth certificate. I had nothing to worry about. They had no children of their own yet and had been wanting to adopt a baby. My body became a factory to produce one for them.

I got fatter and fatter and I weighed 180 lbs at delivery. The doctor kept me calm with pills and notes of excuses. All I did was study, eat, and attend lectures. I had to drop four of my classes, but with the doctor's notes, I would be allowed to retake them the following year. I was a mess. You would not have known that only five months before, a child genius with a dancer's body lived in the clothes I then wore (the few that fit me). I gave up ballet for good.

After the second semester, I spent my break time at the dorm, pretending to take some of my make-up classes.
The *father* and *mother-to-be* were happy. As far as I was aware, his wife had no idea that the father of that little baby I was carrying was her own husband. I delivered the baby in their own apartment. After the birth, the wife took the baby to another room. I never even got to see it until hours later. The doctor assisted with the delivery. Father. He cleaned me up and put me into a small bed in the spare room of their apartment. Then, he left me alone. Totally alone, as he joined his new child and his wife. I wanted to scream from anguish, from something!

'Somebody, listen to me! Things are not what they seem to be! Listen, somebody hear me! Please!' My heart was silently shouting in the dark. Hours later, I heard the door open. I must have dozed off, because I was startled and for a moment, I couldn't tell where I was. Then, I saw the doctor come into the room, holding the tiny bundle wrapped in a blanket.

"Be careful with him," he said, as if I were some by - stander, waiting for her turn to fondle his child!

"It's my baby. I took care of it for the last nine months!" When I held the tiny little thing to my chest, I still had no idea if it was a boy or a girl. No one had told me.
I had to check for myself! 'A boy! I gave birth to a son!'
I thought. As soon as I held him, he began to nuzzle me.
I started to cry. He was so small! He was born three weeks too soon, and he came in a hurry. He must have been around five pounds at the most. I don't know, I never knew. Right then all I knew, that I had every one of my emotions going through my mind and my body. Every feeling I ever could have or had were shooting through me, all at the same time.

"Take him now!" I remember having yelled and then I passed out.

"...We named him Robert," was all I heard. When I regained consciousness, I made a promise to myself: 'I am going to get out of here. Out of this place, out of this country, away from these people! Whatever I may do in my life, it will not be in this country, with these kinds of people! I'll get out of here, somehow!'

I had a secret, which only three people knew of. At the age of thirteen and a half, I gave birth to a little boy named Robert. How we kept it a secret, still eludes me.
I nursed my son for six months, mornings and evenings.
Slowly, I shoved my emotions down, deep down, one by one.
I did not lose any of the weight that I gained. I purposely stayed fat and got fatter. I did not want to be beautiful, ever again.

I saw Robert often, even after I stopped nursing him. He called me 'Auntie'. The most painful word I've ever heard. He was two months short of four years old, when I disappeared from his life. Forever. He never called me 'Mama.'

Laci stuck with me, though he received his diploma six months before I received mine. He came to see me at my graduation. He was still the most beautiful man I ever had seen. I was still fat, with a secret. Years after I left the country I wrote to him and confessed about the baby. It turned out, he knew it all along!

I went from a small town to a big city, hoping to find that nameless, unrecognizable something that I had lost some time ago. I never found it there. Instead, I had learned about *The Beauty and The Beast.*

Chapter 9

Step by Step

I continued to eat, study, attend my lectures and play the game of hide and seek. Manipulation. The doctor supplied me with my sleeping pills for my nights and wake up pills for my mornings. I went back to drinking wine *socially,* not much.

I got elected as secretary of the youth movement.
I was never interested in politics, nor did I understand it.
I often remembered the times when my father was detained for various reasons, sometimes for several days at a time. When he returned home, he was often badly beaten. One of such beatings finally caused him the sight in one of his eyes. *'Political reasons'* - they said. His name was printed in the local newspapers as one of the *disciplined* and kids in school would point their fingers at me. And of course my father would pass those beatings onto me. No, I did not need politics. I had plenty of it attached to my bottom, already! Still, I accepted my nomination (we didn't have a choice) with pretended joy, all along wondering how I would one day use it to my advantage. *Freedom*! On the night of my son's birth I made a promise and I would keep it. *Freedom*!   I planned, I connived and I manipulated.   I studied and ate, drank and smoked. My grades were getting better. I started to earn the respect of my teachers and other students. I took my pills and focused all I could on *freedom*! Secretly, I lived for that one word alone!

I was sent, as an exchange student to four different countries. Each time I returned faithfully and with honors.
I focused on my freedom. In the second semester of my third year I concentrated my studies to psychology and logic. I wanted to study neuro -surgery, but I was turned down. Too young and a female. No! I kept thinking about my freedom. I had no idea how but I new that one day I

would defect to the U.S. I was a plump, sweet genius on the outside, a shrewd, driven, manipulating, hateful defector in the inside. Each day brought me closer to my goal.

I played the game. One of my uncles was a communist and I befriended him. He taught me a few things about the system. Like eager beavers, they were all ready to help me. I hated them all, which came easily since most of them were men. I had no real reason to think that I ever could, but I knew that I will make my freedom happen. I will leave someday. I let them *help* me, but after only three months I was removed from my position. It seemed I was under qualified, after all. I didn't give up!

Sometime, in 1963 friends of my parents' who lived in America came to visit their relatives and us. Fat or not, they liked me and one day the woman asked if I would ever consider visiting them in New York, if she sent me a plane ticket. Would I ?!?!

"I would really like that," I replied coyly, finding it difficult to keep my excitement under control. We didn't talk any more about it, so I kept my burning desire to smolder under cover. *Freedom*! It was all I could dream about. A chance at freedom, my first chance at freedom!
I still hadn't said a word to anyone. It was just another one of my secrets.

I often wondered what will become of my son. I had such deep pain in my heart that I sometimes felt it physically tighten. He will never be my son. He could never be! It hurt so bad to think that I will leave him behind. Yet, I knew that I must. I visited him often. Robert was a beautiful little boy. He had learning difficulties and he developed slower than average, I noticed but did not ever talk to his father about it. By the time he was two, they cut back on my visits to him, insisting that I spend more time on my studies. Little by little, he became less and less mine and more and more theirs. The emotional numbness returned and eventually I shoved it behind the door of the dark room with all the other emotions and pain of my past.

From time to time I would have terrible nightmares and I would bolt up in bed in the middle of the night, tears running down my face, yet I never could remember what the dream was about. Nor did I make any sound, just sit straight up and be a total blank. Often the dream and waking up would reoccur at least twice a night. Still, I'd be silent, never waking up my roommates.

I took my pills - blue in the evenings and pink in the mornings. I partied once or twice with my roommates, their current boyfriends and Laci. He was still around, still my friend. I never confessed to him, though. I didn't trust anyone. We did most everything together, from studying to research, to working on papers and reports or going to see movies. The only thing he disapproved of was my smoking, a habit I cultivated from the day I knew for sure that I was pregnant. If my fatness bothered him, he never said so. Still, however wonderful he was I couldn't see beyond the fact that he was one of them: a man.

I struggled through my teenage years, stuck among adults, not learning how to do either teenage or adult things. I was numb emotionally, save for my burning hate toward men and my unquenchable thirst for freedom.
I wanted to be anyone else, anywhere else but who or where I was at.
One day, in the spring of 1965 I received a letter from the people in New York. I was asked if I would like to visit America during that summer! Would I! At spring break I rode the train home to talk to my parents. They didn't care, in fact they liked the idea. I was about to get my degree in June or so anyway, so why not? I suppose they thought it would delay my coming home to live with them.
My mother took over the details of the arrangements and on the very last day of June, 1965 I received a round trip ticket to New York, USA, via Pan American Airlines!!
I was bursting with joy and I wanted to shout from one end of the country to the other! Instead, I kept silent and waited

for my graduation day to come on July 5, 1965. The departure date on the ticket said: July 7, 1965. I had only two days to get ready to leave!

Laci came to celebrate my victory of graduation. No one else did. I was seventeen and a half years old, graduating from college and nobody from my family came to show they cared. It made no difference to them. *I made no difference to them!* I was deeply hurt.

I didn't mention a word to Laci about my trip.
I didn't go to the party to celebrate, either. Instead, I took the electric street car to see my son for the last time. I held him in my arms, choking on my emotions. When a tear fell from my eye, his little finger reached up to wipe it away. My heart was breaking and I thought my mind would explode.

"Auntie," he said and held my face between his tiny palms and with a smile on his sweet face he gave me a kiss. I told him that I loved him and that I would be going away. He didn't understand me. He was an autistic child and I was the only one with whom he ever calmed down. I wanted to take him with me but I knew that it was impossible. I kissed him good-bye and all I could say to him was:

"Please, forget me." He was almost four years old,
I was seventeen and a half. I have in my memory a picture of his sweet face, his beautiful green eyes, his loving smile and most tender touch which no one can ever erase.

The rest of the afternoon I spent with Laci. He wanted to come with me to wherever I was going earlier in the day but I didn't let him. He never complained about it, nor did he ever question my whereabouts all those times when I could not be found.

The afternoon was ours and we held hands and walked through the city to all the places we spent time together during the last four years. He was still beautiful, gentle and quiet. He was almost twenty three years old. My one and only friend and he still didn't know anything about me. It was best that way. When we got to our favorite island, we walked into one of the gardens and sat on the

110

lawn. He lay me into his lap and looked as though he wanted to say something. I never gave him a chance.

I began to cry, laying there on his lap under the heat of the early July sun. He cradled me without a word and rocked me as if I were a baby. I kept crying. Anguished and full of fear, looking forward to leaving yet terrified of the very thought of it. I wanted so much to tell him about my trip, but I didn't. When my cry calmed and my normal breathing had returned, I said to him as I looked into those eyes that started so much confusion in me four and a half years before:

"I still feel like I'm only thirteen years old. Will I ever grow up? Is it hard to grow up?"

"Baba, you are more grown up than any other woman I know." He wiped a tear away.

"Woman? Believe me, I'm far from being a woman. I'm just big! Not grown up, just big!" I was depressed. Laci looked down at me, slightly shook his head and smiled.

I just had to ask him:

"Why did you stick around me all those years? I need to know. I never understood it and in the back of my mind I always felt uneasy about it. Some other places in my mind I felt good." After a short time he took a deep breath and said:

"You don't know you as I know you. You try so hard to be a mystery woman. You try to shelter yourself from everybody, most of all from your own self. One day you will understand it all."

"Was this your way of saying: I don't know?"

"What will you do now that its all done? Where will you run to?"

"Run? Why do you say that?"

"Is this your way of saying: I don't know?"

Tears came to my eyes at the thought of leaving him. How could I tell him that in only two days I am going to be gone for ever? I didn't think he'd understand it. I couldn't stay it. There is nothing here that is mine, no place I belong to anymore. No shelter to hide behind or under. Even though Laci was right there, I felt alone.

No one else cared to come and watch me walk down that long isle which represented more struggle, more fear, more pain to me than anyone can ever imagine. I was not a whiz-kid anymore, only a fat, struggling kid. I was average. I learned a lot and fought a lot, for what? I was raped and broken again and I bleed from my soul more than from my body. Seventeen and a half years filled with pain, confusion, and emptiness . Monsters attacking in my sleep in the darkness of the night. No, I cannot stay here.

"I will write to you." That was all I could say.

In my *dysfunction* I was outstanding, which blossomed later in life.

Once at home, I packed, informed my parents of my trip and spent the next day and a half with my brother. He was then twelve years old. He and I walked over to my grandmother's little farm. In the privacy of her small but breathtakingly beautiful flower garden, under a huge black walnut tree, I tried to tell her, without saying the words out loud that I will not come back. She understood me. She said that in her heart I will always be her little wondering bird, her *little sparrow.* That enduring, strong yet fragile, beaten and misunderstood little creature of God. She was the only one who spoke to me of God ever in my tender life.

I loved that little woman more deeply than any other person ever alive, until recent years. She was my giant, my mentor, my breathe of life. She was my unconditional love and constant affirmer.

It is important to note, that I did not speak a word of English at that time. Yet, I was ready to take the journey across the ocean to a country, a culture I knew nothing about. I was ready to leave everything and everyone behind to find my freedom and start over again. At seventeen and a half years of age I didn't realize that I had only one burden. A burden that kept traveling with me no matter where I went. It was my constant companion, the cause of my shadow. *Me.* I was the burden which I was trying to run away from yet could never lose or leave behind. I was my own burden for forty two years.

I spent my last night at my grandmother's farm. We didn't talk but stayed close together. I slept in her bed, feeling her crippled, arthritic finger smooth my red hair. She was humming a tune I hadn't yet heard her sing before. I felt love pouring out from her entire being and I soaked it up. My last night at home I felt safe and secure. My only night. For years to come, I used the memory of the fullness of my feelings that night. We said good-bye in the silent serenity of our spirits.

In the morning I awoke early. My anxiety wore on me and I wanted to get going before someone could stop me and put an end to my dream. My mother came to see me and with her she brought a small package. Her last gift to me. I didn't even look at it. She put it neatly into my suitcase, then tightened the straps around it. My father did not come and he didn't seem to send any message, either. Just as well. I had never seen him alive again. My brother cried and whispered into my ear:

"Don't be too long, please. I'll miss you."

I took the train all alone, heading for a new life to somewhere where the world was filled with goodness, freedom and all the things I didn't have. Peace. I wanted peace. Before heading to the airport, I decided to stop at the doctor's apartment and ask him for more pills. I was lucky, he was at home. He was alone. My son and his wife were out. I wanted desperately to see my son one more time, but it didn't happen. My heart ached.

When the doctor returned with the two small bottles, I just laughed.

"Those won't be enough. You see, I am going away for a while and I need at least a year's supply!"

"Huh? What do you mean you're going away? Where are you going for so long?" He almost sounded relieved.

"Its not your concern. Your concern is to give me the pills and I promise you that you will never have to see me again. That's what you've been wanting all along! Well, your wish is about to come true. Your secret will never be out of the closet. You will never have to worry about what I say or do, ever again. I promise you. But I need enough pills to last me until I find another doctor. A doctor, who will not rape me." I felt that he deserved those words!

"Fine." I could not believe he agreed so easily. I was relieved. He left the room for a few minutes and when he returned, he had my pills in two large bottles with him. He handed them to me and I stuffed the two bottles into my handbag, having no idea how I am I going to get them through customs. I took one last, long look at him and remembered the very first appointment I had with that man. In the beginning I was filled with terror, then I trusted him, needed him, believed in him. I needed to believe in something. But he raped me and blamed me for what he did. Why? I lost the last ounce of childhood that was left in me. I could never get that back. Right there he stood, in front of me, the father of my son whom he took away from me because I couldn't take care of my own baby. I hated that man for hurting me with the same passion and intensity I hated my father. I turned around and without a word, walked away. I firmly shut the door behind me for extra measure. Just once, only once I needed to hear my son say: 'Mama'. He never did.

I went through customs without a baggage check. The officer just stuck a label on both pieces and I was told to board right away. Within a half hour the airplane door was shut tight and I sat in my seat in a conscious coma. 'What am I doing?' I asked myself. Suddenly, I realized that for the first time in my life, I finally received what I yearned for. More than anything in the world, I wanted to get away from my life and here I was, doing it.

As I remember back to that time, sitting inside of the vehicle which was about to transport me into a brighter future, I had no fear of a usual kind. I was eager to get going and I kept repeating the reassuring words of my own: 'Whatever will be, will be...everything is going to be fine...there is no going back now...just look ahead and you'll be fine...everything will be fine..' The aircraft took off, lifted and I left the land of my birth. I was hoping that I left everything else in my life behind, also.

It was not to be.

*At my father's funeral, I spoke to him in English,
so no one would understand me.*

Part II

Chapter 1

A Desire Fulfilled?

There was no one waiting for me at Kennedy Airport as I arrived in New York, USA. Since I spoke no English and had no US money, my immediate destiny did not look very bright. At one hundred and eighty pounds and only five feet six inches tall I did not make a physical impression which would have caused a great deal of positive interest in others.

I waited around for the friends of my family to arrive, snatch me away and bring me to safety in my new found freedom. Nothing. Finally, after hours of pacing, sitting and standing, I handed the only piece of information I had in my possession - the address and phone number I had been given by my mother, along with the name of the people I came to be with - to a uniformed man standing behind the counter under the words: PAN AM. He smiled and went into a long speech of what I thought to be a series of questions. I smiled back to him, shrugged my shoulders and shook my head. He smiled even wider and began to speak the same unintelligible language to me, this time so slowly, one would have thought that there was something wrong with him. When he was done he stopped, looked at me with his eyes wide open, waiting for me to do something. I did. I smiled back at him, opened my eyes wide, shook my head again and shrugged my shoulders deep and long. And we understood that we did not understand each other. Then he motioned with his hands, which to me meant 'stay right here' and disappeared with my paper, behind a door. When he returned I was still standing in the same spot. He brought with him another person, a woman. They both spoke English to me and in reply I shrugged my shoulders to both of them. Instead of two, now we had three frustrated people stuck in a situation we didn't know how to solve. I had a small white purse in my hand and the woman motioned to me to hand it over to her. I put the purse up on the counter. In my homeland, we were constantly stopped and searched through our personal effects by the military, so to me this was not out of the ordinary. The woman opened the purse and found my passport which identified my origin and language we hoped someone in their system also spoke. Bingo! Within a few minutes I was jabbering along, expressing my need, fear and frustrations. They contacted the people I needed to be with and two hours later I was sitting inside of a huge Buick, gaping at the skyscrapers of Manhattan.

It was late in the evening already and dark outside. The city was lit up like a huge Christmas tree, flickering in the night from all directions. I had never seen anything so beautiful before and I fell speechless at the wonder of the magnitude it imposed on my mind!

'This is my new home and so far, I am the only one that knows it.' I thought. 'I am finally here. Now I simply have to figure out a way to stay here,' was my next thought.

The area of the city where these people lived, who in the following few days became my Godparents, was called Yorktown, in Manhattan, NY. They owned the big old Brownstone building, and once we were inside, I was put into a matchbook size room, suitcase and all. As I unpacked my baggage, I found the presents my mother placed into it: they were ten packs of cigarettes and a bottle of very fine and expensive brandy. I smiled in relief and put them away at the bottom of one of the drawers of the dresser. Then, I pulled out the presents I knew were meant for me to give to them and we visited for a little while. After a short explanation of my airport experience we all went to sleep. They seemed to have been proud of me for not falling apart from fear.

In the middle of the night I bolted straight up in bed as I awoke from a nightmare. My body, my bedding was drenched in sweat and my heart pounded. I couldn't remember the nightmare that woke me up. I began to silently cry from anguish, anger and total disappointment:

'Why don't you leave me alone, whatever you are! I just left everything behind and you were supposed to stay behind, too! Why can't you leave me alone! I want to be free of you. Free! Leave me alone!' I lay back down onto the soaked bed and cried and cried and cried. Until I fell asleep.

Through the following few months I was kept busy. I went to the United Nations and talked with people, seeking help with my defection. My Godparents had the idea of my permanent stay also, so after brief exchanges of ideas we relaxed in agreement. They dragged me around the city shops and department stores for more suitable and fashionable clothing. My Godmother was determined to turn me into an instant American. I didn't protest. I noticed that my fatness was outstanding. I made up my mind to get rid of my excess weight. I didn't fit in with the young Americans' looks and I was determined to fit in!

I was brought to church for Catholic worship which I did not understand. I was introduced to friends, friends of friends, families and families and friends of families. I was busy. I listened to meaningless gossip about the lives of people I didn't meet yet, but was assured that I would. I was introduced to men, eligible men, young and old.

My visa was expiring in three months and I was denied an extension. Back to the U.N.

I was introduced to more eligible men and finally one day a comet hit my conscious awareness. It came in a form of many words from the mouth of my new Godmother:

"You will have to get married. That's the only way," said she.

"Huh? To whom?" I asked her. There were several willing prospects, I was told and there was still one more person whom I didn't meet yet, a problem that was soon corrected.

This young man was twenty four years old, had recently returned from the Air Force and was ready to settle down. He was looking for a woman from my homeland. Lucky me!

"What happened to defecting?" I asked in desperation.

"You defect later, you get married now!" I listened in disbelief. 'I haven't even found my freedom, yet,' Ithought.

"Listen Sweetheart, this boy is also our Godchild. He comes from a nice family. You've already met and like his father and he's crazy about you. Once you've met the son, you'll think differently. He's very handsome, too."
I heard the assuring ways of caring adults who knew what was good for me. It was true, I already met and liked the father. That was all.

Well, we met, Mick and I. He was nice, fun, tall and average looking. (Nothing like Laci, though!) We were given several opportunities to date, to get together and we did. His father liked me. His mother, who hadn't met me yet, hated me. I learned, that for many years there had been a family feud between her and my Godmother, therefore I became a new object for her negative thoughts and wishes. Mick's parents were divorced long ago which made matters even less comfortable.

Still, we rushed into full-time dating and in October of 1965, four and a half months after my arrival to the United States, I found myself walking down the isle of a Greek Catholic church to be married to a young man I barely new.

I had a pretty good idea of what I was doing. Even though I was terrified and secretly hoped that an angel would fly over me and scoop me up and snatch me away,

I accepted the idea and settled with it.

The church was relatively full with members of the congregation, most of whom had been friends of either my Godparents or my Father-in-law. I had no one there to wish me well or happy.

I said: "I do". I was not yet eighteen years old. I was sad and afraid of the unknown. I also knew that for the time being, I was secure.

The joy and wonder of the honeymoon ended shortly and abruptly after the wedding. Mick's mother came to visit us frequently and always unannounced, which angered my husband greatly. They would fight and I'd get in the middle of it, trying to keep quiet and peace between them. Then, they would both turn against me for being the cause of it all. His mother would run out of the apartment in hysterical cries and Mick would hit me.

Life was getting to be just like it used to be, when I was a little girl.

I started to take my blue and pink pills again, after I discovered the same old pain returning from my insides. I started to wake up and bolt upright in the middle of the night more and more frequently. Mick complained that I was disturbing him. I cried more often than not, usually for no apparent reason. Mick would be upset, yell and call me awful names, most of which I had yet to understand. All of that went on for about a year after we were married. By then I had lost close to eighty pounds, which also annoyed my new husband.

My Father-in-law came to visit me one day when I was at home, alone. He seemed to sense the trouble in our lives and said he wanted to help me. At first I kept listening to him as he tried to assure me that he really wanted to help and since we were family, it was O.K. for me to turn to him for help. I opened up to him and cried and cried for what felt like forever. He comforted me, gave me some wine and listened quietly as I poured out my trouble filled soul to him about my husband, his ex-wife and my marriage.

"You poor child! You must be very lonely. I know that you feel unloved. I had no idea that things were that bad! I'm going to give that son of mine a big piece of my mind, you just wait and see! How could he be so cruel to you! You are such a *good girl!* He should love you, like I love you! Oh, you are such a *good girl,* you deserve the best! Wait 'til I get a hold of him! I'll teach him how to treat you!" He was angry with his son. I was afraid of his son!

"Oh, please don't say anything to him, please! He'll be even more angry at me for talking to you!" I pleated with my Father-in-law and started to cry again.

"Hush, hush, little one. I am only going to show him how to love you. He just doesn't know how to love a good girl like you," he went on petting my hair, rocking me back and forth. "I love you so much Honey, I don't want anything to happen to you. It's O.K., Honey. Shh. I love you. You are a *good girl.* I love you." He poured some more wine for me and kept telling me how much he loved me... then he showed me how much... he loved me...he loved me more that he had to...more than he should have.

I didn't say a word to Mick. I had another secret, another man - *someone I once trusted* - to hate.

My marriage lasted two and a half years. I left Mick on the day he threw a knife at me and pushed me against the radiator and the bridge of my nose broke. I moved in with a woman I worked with at a Garden City ladies' fashion store. The two of us rented a small, furnished apartment on Fire Island and she drove us to work each morning.

I had new immigration problems. It seemed that my political involvement - during the three brief months in my school years - were working against me. The very thing that got me out was about to keep me out! I was worried about being deported. Whatever little contribution I made to the supposed betterment of our youth was now standing in my way. It took me nearly twelve years to finally earn my American citizenship. I discussed my immigration dilemma with my new roommate. I figured that being a bonified American and an older woman (she was twenty three), she would have all the answers.

"You'll have to get pregnant and have a baby. They can't kick you out with an American baby!" Words of wisdom from the older woman.

I couldn't talk to Mick, because by that time he didn't really care too much about me. I had drifted away from my Godparents to keep some kind of peace with my Mother-in-law. The only person that I could turn to was my Father-in-law. I called him.

"Baba, this is going to come as a big shock to you, but even if you and Mick stayed together you would not have been able to get pregnant. Mick can't have any children. Not with you, not with anyone else. You see, when he was down in Central America he contracted malaria and do to the high fever that he had, he became sterile. I'm so sorry that you didn't know this sooner."
I wondered: 'How much more is there that I was not aware of and should have been?' It didn't matter anymore.

I kept thinking about what my life could be with a baby, but I had very little experience in stable family function, so I just made believe how things could or should be. I could raise a child and not do all those terrible things to him or her as I was done to. I painted a heavenly lovely mental picture of our lives. Mommy and Baby. I wrote my own fairy tale.

And so the search for the perfect daddy began. My roommate and I frequented bars after bars in our research. Finally, about two weeks into this journey, I spotted a remarkably handsome young man. He was a musician, a drummer and he played in one of the bands of a bar that we stopped in. I put an end to our wandering around and concentrated on that particular bar and we became regulars. The legal drinking age at that time in New York

State was eighteen, so I was a legal drinker in 1967. A few days passed and I met the drummer face to face. He was captivated by my accent and looks. He was very good looking off stage, also. With those qualities, we had filled the requirements to start a meaningful relationship. His name was Michael.

Michael was fun and funny, with the hot temper of an artist. I was fascinated by him and his inexhaustible energy.

Though our relationship was very short lived, he did leave me with the most beautiful little girl any mother would want to give birth to. Kelly. Soon after I got pregnant, I stopped going to the bar and I left Michael as well, without saying a word to him. In all honesty, I would have liked to create some kind of stable life with Michael, but I didn't know how to do that. All I had was yearning, no experience. I slipped out of sight before he could figure out how massed up I really was.

Kelly was born in September, 1968. Life became very, very difficult for Kelly and. Though I had a good job and worked through my pregnancy up to the day of delivery, we never seemed to get too far. Bills were piling up high and my roommate kicked me out of our tiny apartment. We were homeless and broke. I called Mick for help. He took us back for a while (for the baby's sake), but there was no way for us to even think about recreating a relationship that should never had been in the first place. Kelly and I moved in with another friend, a woman who still is my best female friend today. We were homeless, Kelly and I and we didn't have a lot to claim as our possession. Just the two of us.

My friend lived in Harlem, New York, so when Kelly was only two months old, we joined my friend Nancy in Harlem. One would think that a white and definitely dysfunctional one hundred and four pound foreign woman with a tiny infant would be an easy target for trouble. Not at all. In fact, up to that time, we were probably safer there than we had been anywhere else. My neighbors were

Kelly's baby-sitters. They simply loved her and treated her like a precious jewel. Each evening, someone from the building came to meet me at the subway station as I was coming home from work. We were guarded and protected and our safety became the block's obsession. God save whoever even tried to talk to me!

Nancy and I catered to *our little daughter* and we played house. But I was lonely and I felt guilty for taking off on Michael as I did. One day I telephoned him and somehow I found a way to tell him that he had a daughter. I asked him not to be angry with me and tried to reassure him that I was not expecting anything from him. I told him how deeply I loved our little baby and how she was the focus and purpose of my life. Michael wanted to meet her and came to visit one day. After a while, I decided to leave father and daughter alone.

My friend Nancy and I drove over to visit a friend of hers in New Jersey. We were going to be gone for two, but not more than three hours. On the way back from Elizabeth's, Nancy's car broke down. It was already evening and dark and we were nowhere near home. There was no phone around and I began to worry.

Six hours later we were still in New Jersey, in a middle of the ugliest verbal fight I had experienced with a woman! By two o'clock the following morning, I was close to loosing my mind. Nancy refused to talk to me and I knew that our relationship as roommates had ended. Finally, around 2:30 AM I was able to hitchhike into New York City and I arrived at home close to three in the morning. Michael was furious and Kelly was screaming. Having had no experience with babies, he didn't know what to do. Kelly was soiled and needed her diaper changed hours before! She was hungry and overtired. Before storming out of the apartment, Michael screamed at me for the last time:

"If you ever need a baby-sitter again, don't call me! If you need anything at all, don't ever call me again!" And with

those words he slammed the door behind himself.
I never saw him again.

A few days later my then ex-Father-in-law called and told me that Michael got killed in a car accident. I cried and cried and cried for weeks. I'm not sure why and I'm certain I wasn't sure why, then either. I had hardly known Michael but in some strange way, I loved him. He was the father of my child. Whatever little time we spent together was better than any time I had spent with most other people before him. Hot tempered as he was, until that last night of the broken down car, he had always been gentle and kind to me. Part of me felt as though I used him to father my child. Part of me loved him the best way I knew how.

I never said anything negative to anyone about Michael, including my daughter Kelly. She grew up believing that her father was a gentle, funny and beautiful man. I never married Michael and I never felt ashamed because of it, nor did I ever lie to anyone about it.

My ex-Father-in-law, once again came to my rescue and helped us move out of Harlem and into Brooklyn. I let him. In three years I moved five times. Life was busy.

Many years later, as I reflected back to that part of my past, I wondered how I survived my struggles and troubles. I had the notion that my ex Father-in-law secretly hoped that Mick and I would re-marry. It would have given him the opportunity to be closer to the baby and me. Well, that didn't happen, either. He was very careful not to be alone with me and he never again treated me less than respectful. The damage was done however and neither of us felt completely comfortable near the other. I know
I didn't. I didn't trust him. In fact, I know that I hated him also, along with all those other men who abused me long before.

Shortly after Kelly and I moved to Brooklyn, he died of diabetes. He asked me to come and see him at the hospital. I went. I barely recognized him. He lost much too much weight and he was already very weak. When he saw me in his room, he reached out and took my hand and with tears in his eyes he asked me to forgive him. I did.

That night, just before midnight he passed away.

I was not allowed to go to the funeral. By then, everyone knew that Mick was not Kelly's father. I was a shameful and soiled woman, not to be allowed to enter a Catholic Church.

God discriminated against this little sinner.

There was magic in the sunlight and
I sometimes felt my body heal.

Chapter 2

On My Own

Our little Brooklyn apartment was above a grocery store and we shared our lives with hundreds of roaches. Kelly's crib was constantly covered with a large gauze to keep the roaches from falling down off of the ceiling and on to her. I hated our place but I had no choice but stay in it.

I kept it as clean as I could with the energy I had left after my bouts with depression. Each day I put on my best clothes and attitude, rode the subway to Manhattan and went to work at Bloomingdale's. Kelly had a young mother for a baby-sitter and we did the best we could. After work

I rode the subway back home, picked up the baby and dragged ourselves up the two flights of stairs to find it dark, smelly and filled with a new colony of roaches. My depression increased and I cried more than not. I would feed Kelly her dinner and hold and rock her in my arms while my tears poured over both of us. Often she would cry with me to keep me company, I guessed. Then, she would fall asleep and I'd put her in her crib under the gauze to keep her safe from the bites of those horrid roaches. I'd sit on the only other piece of furniture I had, which was a single bed that I arranged to look like a sofa.

I covered up my head with the sheet and I would rock myself and just keep crying until I too, fell into a fitful and exhausting sleep. My nightmares returned but I still could not remember them when I awoke. I had long ran out of pills, both blue and pink. From time to time I allowed myself to think of my son, the little boy I left behind. There was an echoing ache that thundered inside of my entire being. I felt fearful, alone and lonely, guilty, shameful, angry and filled the rest of the empty spaces with hate.

I hated everyone but my son and daughter. And my grandmother. Them I knew I loved very deeply.

I hated myself and thought of suicide. The only thing that stopped me from going through with it was the thought of leaving Kelly helplessly alone or in the hands of some awful strangers. There was no one to take care of the baby. I started drinking again and heavily.

I had a nice, clean sales job at Bloomingdale's, which was a burden, too. I had to fake being in a good, cheerful mood every day and make other women look and feel better and more beautiful than I ever could, myself. For some special customers I even modeled the clothes they were not sure they wanted in the first place!

On my twenty first birthday I collapsed at work and had to be taken to the emergency room - I don't remember which of hospital. After examination, I was told to take a rest, slow down and relax. I was under - nourished, over stressed and on a verge of a breakdown. As I listened, I inwardly wondered if anyone in that hospital had the slightest idea of what I was feeling or thinking. No matter, I was given six little blue pills and a prescription for more. I was placed back on my old tracks.

Nancy came to visit on one weekend and we talked for a long time. She spent the night with me on the tiny bed which we had to share. When I woke up, she was cooking breakfast for us. She had left the apartment silently, so she would not wake me up, gone downstairs to do some food shopping and returned just as quietly . She was preparing breakfast by the time I awoke. She had already cleaned and fed Kelly. I hadn't rested quite so well in years and she'd let me. I missed her and her unusual Chamorro ways and traditions. She had come from Guam a long time before and now worked for the telephone company. For many years, she was married to the son of the Godparents I had lived with at the beginning of my American life. Nancy had five children, all of them living with their father. Though her ex-husband would have disagreed with me, in my vision she was a wonderful and loving woman. Gentle and caring, kind and good hearted. Although not particularly tidy, she more than made up for that lack by her loving nature and sunny personality. She was and still is the only and best female friend I ever had or could ask for. She didn't judge me or withhold her love from me for any reason, ever.

"I wrote a letter to my parents." I confessed to her as we sat on the floor eating our breakfasts.

"Really? When? What did you say?"

"Oh, a couple of months ago. I was scared to do it but I did it anyway. At first, I didn't know what to say. It's been four years since I left and neither of us heard of the other. I wasn't even sure if they would get my letter."
I paused for a second then continued:

"You're not going to believe this, but I asked them if I could come back home with Kelly... I don't know Nancy, I can't take this life anymore. I'm so alone and I'm so tired. I'm always crying and I don't have anybody to turn to or to talk to. I'm scared and lonely and I don't know how to be an American mother. I work so hard to have nothing!" My tears were pouring from my eyes right into my eggs.

"I know you are, Baba, I know you are. I used to be, too. But things will get better. They always do. What would you do if you went back home, anyway? Aren't you afraid of being shot anymore?" Nancy looked at me with her deep brown eyes, her face expressing honest concern.

"Well, I didn't care about that anymore I just needed to know that Kelly would be safe and taken care of. Anyway, it doesn't matter now."

"What do you mean?" asked Nancy.

"Here, read it yourself." I handed her the only letter I had ever received from my father.

"I can't read this, Sweets, it's not written in English."

"Oh. Here, I'll translate for you. It says:

'Dear Daughter,

Your mother and I were surprised to hear from you after all these years. Very surprised. Much has happened, since you left us which you are not aware of and I don't want to complain to you about, now. It's enough for you to know that your family suffered much pain and hardship because of your defecation, especially since you showed no loyalty for the wonderful things which your native country had given to you. We are getting older and as you know, we are not rich people. It is not reasonable for you to expect your old parents to take care of you and a new baby, too. The truth is Baba, you made your own bed, now you have to lay in it.

Good luck.

Father!'

I finished with a broken soul.

"You must be hurting very deeply," said Nancy quietly. With a quick slide on the floor she sat next to me and held me close in her arms.

"Go ahead, it's O.K. to cry. I'm here for you." She assured me of her loving support.

"I don't have any tears left. Wanna know what's funny? My father is only forty six years old and my mother is forty nine. I hope I won't be too old for Kelly when I reach that age." We set quietly on the floor with our backs against the wall and I wandered: 'Where did all the roaches go during the day?' There was not even one to be seen.

"Nancy, I wrote another letter, also. I wrote to Laci." I said after a while.

"Did you?" was all she said.

"Yes. He also answered. Not like my father, though. He wrote a very long letter. He was glad to hear from me and he said to come back and he'd take care of both of us. Nancy, he knew all about my pregnancy, my son, all of my troubles through school. He was waiting so that one day I would tell him. He said he was very, very hurt, because

I left without a word. Because I didn't trust him. But it wasn't about trust! I didn't tell him about coming to America because I didn't want him to get into trouble with the government! Still, he wants us to go back home. I sent him a picture of us, you know. And guess what? He sent me one of himself. Wanna see it?" I asked my friend with a hopeful smile.

"Sure." My purse was hanging on the doorknob of the closet door and I lifted it off. I reached in, knowing exactly where to find it and I looked at it before I handed it over to Nancy.

"I'd go back, today!" We both laughed.

"You know Nancy, since that night of my thirteenth birthday when I first met him, well, only in these past few days did I ever really allow myself to think of him as a complete man. Not a boy of eighteen. Not a beautiful boy. Not a nice, quiet, gentle boy but all of it put together. Complete. You see, when we were growing up, I saw him in parts and pieces at different times. First, I saw his beauty. Then I sensed his gentleness. Later I needed his friendship. Do you understand what I mean? Until now, my memory had him in parts and pieces like some biology specimen. And it was fine that way. Now that I am able to better understand the complete man, he scares me. I wouldn't know how to be with someone who is so...you know what I mean. He's so...all there. So together. I'm a bigger mess now than I was at seventeen. I would look absolutely stupid next to him. I'm tired of trying to be the things I'm really not. I've hurt so many people in my life, I can't keep doing it forever. It's nice to know that he'd be there for us, that he is there for us but I know that I'm not good enough for him." I was rapidly depressing myself, something I knew how to do really well.

"You don't think much of yourself, do you, Baba?" Nancy asked as she looked down into her lap.

"Actually, I think about myself quite a lot."
I answered.

"Yes, that you do. But you don't think highly of yourself. You don't like yourself, do you?" She looked deep into my eyes as if she wanted to read my brain through the openings.

"Come on Nancy, tell me what is there to like? Who would want to be with a girl that's done all the things I did? A girl with two children out o' wedlock? No home, no furniture, no car, no family, no friends, no nothing! Answer me! What is there to like! I drink a lot, I smoke two packs of cigarettes a day, I have to take pills to make sense of my days, I wake up in nightmares each night! I'm afraid to go to sleep anymore because I know that the damn dream is there waiting for me to fall asleep so it can torture me!" Emotions unlocked, they now ran freely all over me and my friend. I was drowning in them.

"I wish I knew what to tell you. But I don't. If I had the answers I would have used them to fix my life. As I see it, you have two things going for you, which I don't: You are very beautiful and you have your child with you." Nancy stood up and collected the breakfast plates from our laps. I was speechless. She was right. I had my child with me, she didn't have any of hers with her. People constantly reminded me of how beautiful I was. I didn't see myself that way but it was time to accept it. Nancy was not so pretty on the outside but beautiful on the inside.

We moved about the apartment carefully until I broke the silence:

"Nancy, there is something else. There is something else that Laci wrote. My son, Robert had died on August 23rd, last year. Only five days before his seventh birthday. Only eleven days before Kelly was born." I whispered to my friend.

Nancy dropped a juice glass into the sink, which broke. She didn't say a word. I stared at her back and saw her shoulders move up and down. She was crying. I had no tears left. We kept each other company in the silence of the

morning. Nancy with her thoughts, me within my numbness-
for a very long time. It was I, who broke the silence again:

"My old modeling agency wants me to go back and
work for them. Pay is good and I can pretty much pick my
hours. I can take Kelly to the sets with me. If I have to leave
town, she can come with me, also."

"You sure are full of news today! Why don't you take
it? You were pretty happy there before, weren't you?
I remember you bragging about your boss and his wife."

"The Platters. Yeah. They were the closest to what
I never had and always wanted as parents."

"So? What are you going to do?"

"I'm going back." Kelly squirmed, waking from her
morning nap and I rushed to pick her up. She was such a
happy wake-up-er. She rubbed her ocean blue eyes,
yawned and stretched her little arms up, with a smile,
reflecting her sense of innocence and trust unaffected by
the lack of prosperity around her. She had her Mama.
I held her close to me and kissed the top of her dark, curly
hair covered head. I loved my child. Then my vision
reflected the image of a little boy who never called me
'Mama' and now was gone from my life forever. In a crazy
way I loved my children.

I returned to my old modeling job, creating garment
labels and party hose jackets. The general public has an
image of runway and high fashion models displayed in
magazines. Not everyone makes it to the big times. There
are much more small time models who work just as hard or
harder, who's faces and figures are used for silent, visual
marketing, who's faces and bodies are displayed on various
sizes of paper labels hanging on thousands of garment
sleeves or waist bands, than you could think of. Those
beautiful legs on pantyhose packaging belong to bodies and
faces no one ever sees. I was one of those small time,
seventh avenue unknowns.

I had many different jobs by that time, already.

I started out working in a factory, winding copper wire onto a spool, which somehow turned into a part for transistors. When the foreman squeezed one of my breasts, I got up and walked out of that job. My second job was at another factory where I had to cut layers of knitted fabrics into children's garments. After having an accident when,
I sliced three of my fingers across the knuckles and nearly lost them, I was laid off from work for three months. When
I was allowed to return to work, I got lucky. The house model quit and I immediately replaced her. I liked my new job, tried to be very good at it and I was earning a lot more money than I did before. It amazed me how differently
I was being treated all of a sudden! I didn't stay at that job very long, though. One of the customers, who I modeled some clothes for one day, offered me a job on seventh avenue, in Manhattan. I talked to the owner of the factory about it and he assured me that I was given a wonderful opportunity and I should accept the offer. He said that
I was much too pretty to waste myself in a small factory. So, with his blessings I took the job and worked at it until my troubles with Mick began. I left with the understanding that I could return anytime I'm ready. When I did feel better and was ready, instead of going back to seventh avenue, I took a selling/modeling job in the bridal department of a ladies fashion store and worked there until my labor pains with Kelly began. Soon after Kelly was born, I went to work for Bloomingdale's as a sales girl.
That is where the Platters had seen me again.

The following Monday I called them and received my old job back.

Chapter 3

Charles

Nancy spent more and more time with us. Little by little, my mini home got reasonably furnished. I used my spare time to decorate windows and beds, tables and bathroom. I used colorful sheets and I cut and sewed, pinned and shaped. I wrote to my parents and thanked them for letting me know where we stood with each other. I had to rewrite my letter a few times. My choice of words were not mailable at first but with practice I mellowed out and with Nancy's help I tried to accept them as they were. The letter to Laci was much more difficult and took just as long to compose. I thanked him for all that he was to me in the past and honestly told him what a mess I still was. He deserved to have a life free of all the potential difficulties my return would surely create for him. I sent him more pictures, some from my portfolio clippings. Painfully, I told him that I will stay out of his life, save for a surprise visit, should I ever have a chance to go back home. He didn't answer my letter, and years later, when I did return to my birth place again, as much as I wanted to, I did not look him up, nor did I call. I left things alone.

I went to work almost every day, taking Kelly with me. She no longer needed a sitter, since my manager's wife insisted on keeping the baby with her. I was delighted at seeing how much everyone loved my baby. Sometimes she even set and posed with me. The only difficulty I had was coming home to an empty place. I was lonely for something, for someone.

"Baba, how would you like to meet a friend of mine?" The three of us were walking on the Brooklyn Heights Promenade when Nancy startled me out of daydreaming with her question.

"I'd love to met any of your friends but she can't move in with us. We ran out of room!" I laughed jokingly.

"Don't worry, he won't."

"He?" I looked at Nancy. "Who is he?"

"His name is Charles. I've been talking to him about you. As a matter of fact, he lives only two blocks away from you." She explained.

"Really? Tell me about it."

"I've known him for a long time. We used to work together. Now, he works for the city as a social worker and is about to get his Ph.D. He's Italian, twenty seven, never been married, tall, handsome, dark, and whatever else you might see in him."

"I see," said I. "It sounds more than just meeting a friend of yours. It sounds more like a fix-up with a blind date."

"Hm. It is. I know you'll like him." Nancy was encouraging me to say yes to her plan.

"Oh Nancy, you know how unlucky I am with men. I don't really like them. Actually I kind of resent them. Maybe even hate them in a way. Men and me are trouble together." I thought I was saying no, without actually using the word.

"This guy is different. He's stable."

"Nancy, all men are the same. I am different. I am the one who doesn't know what to do with them. I'm the one who gets messed up and hurt at the end because I don't know how to be a woman!" I pleaded with her, being disappointed in myself.

"Just meet him, you don't have to marry him!"

"O.K., fine! You arrange it!" I was feeling angry and cornered. I wasn't sure if Nancy sensed the change in my mood or not. She didn't seem to show much concern. I turned Kelly's stroller around and headed toward home.

"You... you...you are Manonne, aren't you? Yes, you are! Wow, I can't believe my eyes! A real life model!

I don't know what to say!" A young girl appeared in front of me waving her hands up and down, doing her little dance of excitement in front of my daughter, breathlessly gibbering with a big smile on her face.

"Why don't you just say: Good-bye!" I yelled at the poor girl angrily. When I saw the shock and disappointment on that child's face, I wanted the ground to open up below me and swallow me! How could I have been so rude to someone who only wanted to show me respect by recognizing me? I didn't feel beautiful and I knew I needed some serious training in humility! No, there wasn't very much to like in me, even by a blind date!

"Nancy, com'on, let's go back home. I'll meet your friend if you arrange it, O.K.?" I smiled cautiously and with a lot of guilt.

Charles was everything Nancy described him to be. He had the ability to make me feel at ease. He was reserved, yet had a good sense of humor. Our first date was casual, both of us just coming home from work. We met at a subway station. For our second date he packed a basket for a Prospect Park picnic. French bread, grapes, cheese and wine. My kind o' guy! Charles liked wine.
I loved wine. I liked Charles. Charles thought I was beautiful.

Charles moved us, Kelly and me into his apartment. Charles had a wonderful family: mother, brother and sister. He was the oldest of three children. They spoiled and pampered us. Within ten months Charles and I were married.

Soon after my marriage to Charles life changed again. My immigration difficulties cleared and I became eligible for citizenship. Charles quit his job to find himself. I found out that Charles smoked hashish and pot and I had a hard time finding him among the clouds of smoke.

Each day I took Kelly to the sitter, since I could not trust Charles with her. Charles would be lying on the sofa puffing on his joint. After my sets at work I'd pick Kelly up, bring her and the groceries home and find Charles still lying on the sofa puffing on his water pipe. He'd be talking with old girlfriends about old stuff, not letting onto his married status ,which exasperated me to no end. One day, I got so angry that I yanked the phone out of his hand, introduced myself as his wife and asked the woman on the other end of the line never to call us again.

"Us?" she retorted. "I didn't call *us*, Honey, I called Charles."

"Well *Sweetie,* Charles is now my husband not your boyfriend, and there is no room for you in our lives! So don't call here anymore! Get it!" I slammed down the phone as my husband watched me furious and out of control.

"I like it when you're all fired up." He laughed.

"I'd like it if you got a job! I'm tired of seeing you laying around all day!"

"I'm not laying around, I'm finding myself." Charles looked at me amazed and hurt.

"All you have to do is ask me! You're finding yourself? You're laying on that, that damn sofa day and night puffing on one dope thing or another! You are lost? Babe, all you have to do is ask me! I'll tell you where you are! There you are rotting away on my sofa, you, you lazy bastard! Now get off the phone, get off of my sofa and get a job or get out!" I had enough of him and his smooth, gentle manipulation.

"O.K., if that's what will make you happy? No problem." Charles was calm, I was frantic, shaking and stumbling from the adrenaline overload. He picked up the telephone, dialed some number and after channeling to the right person, said:

"Yes, Sir, I'll accept the position and the terms of your offer. When would you like me to start? Yes, Sir. I'll be there. I look forward to the new challenge and working with you. Good-bye, Sir." He hung up. My mouth dropped open.

140

I was dumb-founded. I didn't know what to say to him. I was even angrier that before. I turned around and left the room.

When I got to the kitchen I found Kelly setting atop of a pile of laundry detergent which she pulled out of the pantry and emptied onto the middle of the floor. Her diaper was off of her and she just sat there with her naked butt buried in the white powder, smiling in victory of her accomplishment. I laughed inwardly and picked her up to wash off her little bottom before the detergent burnt more holes into her to leak out of.

Charles' job took us from Brooklyn to upstate New York, one hundred and fifty eight miles north of where I began. It took me from my job. It took me from Nancy and Charles' family, whom I learned to care about. We bought a small house in the mountains on four acres of land, pine trees and a creek. The house was very old and I went back to inventing new uses for colorful sheets. Bedding sheets in various colors, prints, stripes and dots.

Charles was Charles. In the mornings he drove to work, in the evenings he drove me crazy. I didn't know how to be a wife and he didn't know why. My nightmares returned again and when he asked me about them I couldn't tell him. He didn't believe me when I told him that I honestly did not know or remembered any of them.

I discovered lipstick on his underwear. I was both furious and sorry at the same time. On the last day of our nine months of marriage, I handed him his week's worth of colorful underwear.

"You are going to have to take care of these from now on. And you will have to do it somewhere else. I am what I am and you are what you are. Neither of us are perfect and putting us together does not make perfect, either. Each day of this week I hated you for cheating on me every day. Now I want you to go away before I act out my hate. I don't care where you go, but please go and go right now. Charles had nothing to say in return.

On paper, Charles and I were married for six years but in reality we stayed together for only nine months.

After Charles left, I did everything I could to get even. It didn't occur to me that it was me whom I was punishing, not him. I went on a rampage. I drank and got drunk in public. I took my little blue valiums. I couldn't live without them. When I didn't take them on time, my body would start to shake and tremble. I washed them down with wine. Instead of milk, I used wine in my breakfast cereal. My nightmares left me exhausted, broken and filled with fear.

Late in October of 1970 I discovered a lump in my left breast. I was not yet twenty three years old. I called Nancy. She came up to be with me and together we went to see a doctor in Hudson, New York. From there, I was sent to New York City. I locked up my little house in the mountains and we drove to Nancy's apartment. By that time she lived in midtown Manhattan. Her sister, visiting from Guam stayed with her and took care of Kelly while the two of us went form one doctor to another, one lab to another, one test to another. I was terrified after each test. Finally, I was told that I needed surgery.

"No way! I have to go back to work. I'm a single mother and I am a model. I can't work with parts of me missing! You gotta do something else! You have to find some other way! You gotta understand, I have a two year old baby to take care of! I have to work! Don't you understand! Doesn't anybody hear me! Don't you care?" I was hysterical. The nurse gave me a shot to calm me down. It actually knocked me out.

"There is a place in England..." the doctor started to explain.

"Good. Get me there. Anything, but surgery! I can not give up my body parts yet, Doctor. Please try to understand. Please!" I was mellowed by the drug.

That's when I met Carla. I did go to England, using the money I saved while I was modeling. I went through radiation and chemotherapy. I lost my hair, my energy and sometimes hope. I lost my meals, but I kept Carla's phone number and my breast. When I returned home, I stayed with Nancy and called Carla. Through the woman from Africa, I found God in me and hope for a continued life.

As for finding me? No. That did not happen. My anger and hate along with all the other negative emotions stayed deep - seated for many more years to come.

I returned to my little house. I never modeled after that and I didn't miss it. I wrapped myself up in my daughter, my wine, my valium and my revenge. I desperately hung onto life, only to discover new ways to destroy it. I went from relationship to relationship, with men equally or more dysfunctional than I was. I craved for a normal life only to search for it in places it could never have come from. I dated men to have them fall in love with me, only to dump them. I was a neon billboard advertising self hate, lack of self-esteem, no self-respect. Those who knew how to read the sign responded instantly. I hated all of them for it.

For two years my revenge on the world and myself was unstoppable. Then, Kelly turned four years old and started kindergarten. I went back to school. I decided to study interior design and I traveled to Manhattan, driving the three hundred and sixteen miles each week for four years. After school I went to see Carla every week and surrendered myself to her God - loving way. I stayed as clean as I could but I didn't give my habits up. I simply couldn't. I was hooked, even though I would not have admitted it at the time. I did stay more stable and my focus went to Kelly and my studies.

Chapter 4

Fred

In the summer of 1972 I met, once again a man who became a landmark in my story. Since then I've learned that people attract their own kind, recognizing their own kind, feel comfortable in their discomfort simply because that is all which they can identify with. If you haven't consciously learned something, if you don't have experience with it, you cannot recognize it. It just brushes by you like a summer breeze. You know that it's pleasant but you can't hold onto it. I am not going to detail every lesson I chose to learn from these personal experience. The fact is that nothing, but nothing did ever happen to me which I did not permit on some level of communication.

Fred was from Cuba, a singer and night club entertainer. He romanced me until I said, yes. He spent most weekends with Kelly and I in my mountain home where he loved to come and unwind. The relationship went as far as being asked to marry him, meeting his sister from Florida, getting mixed up with all kinds of dangerous business people who operated questionable wheeling and dealings. During the four years of our relationship I learned that he too, was an alcoholic and hooked on uppers and downers. Who was I to judge?

On the day of my graduation, after receiving my diploma as an interior designer, I decided to drive from Manhattan to Queens, where he had lived and surprise him. There, I was the one who received a surprise. More like a blow or even a shock.

I rang the bell on his door and a woman, dressed in a pink bathrobe, curlers in her hair and an inquisitive look on her face, opened the door.

"Hello, is Fred home?" I asked her with a tremor in my voice.

"No, he's not. I'm not expecting him to come home for another four hours or so." The woman's voice was sharp and she sounded annoyed, even angry.

"May I ask who you are?" I said.

"I'm Barbara, his manager." she answered.

"Do you live here?"

"Yes, I do. And who are you?" She was definitely agitated by then.

"I'm his fiancee. I'm Manonne. Just tell him that I stopped by to say hello." Without looking at her I turned around and walked toward the staircase. My body was trembling and I couldn't stand up any longer. I sat down on a stair step and waited to have a heart attack or something. I felt dizzy and my heart pounded like an army drum signaling for attack. I wanted to cry but my throat was too constricted. I could barely breathe. My head felt like it was going to explode. I felt betrayed. Old, familiar emotions took over my mind and my body responded. Hate! I hated him, I hated myself for believing in the qualities he never had but I chose to put into him because I needed to believe that he had them. I hated myself for fooling myself, I hated myself for needing him. I was in a state of consuming hate! For days and nights to come, I functioned in an awake come. I skipped work and didn't answer my phone. I left Kelly in Manhattan with Nancy and her sister, so she wouldn't see her mom in such a condition.

The same old questions kept flashing through my mind: 'Why? Why do I keep doing the same things over and over again! Why do I keep ending up hurt?' When I finally was able to cry, I went hysterical. I got drunk and took too many valiums. I wanted to die. Having left the lights on all over in my house raised enough alarm in my neighbor to come over and investigate. It was passed midnight when he finally got me to come to enough consciousness where he thought I'd make it.   He didn't call for the police or

146

ambulance. He walked with me all night long while I begged him to let me sleep and leave me alone. The sun was coming up at the top of the mountain when he let me go to bed and fall into a natural sleep.

As I started to answer my phone again, Fred called. He wanted to explain himself and the woman he had lived with all through the four years of our engagement. I listened. I forgave him. Believe it or not, his lies were better than being rejected by someone who didn't know how to respect me, himself or the other woman. His lies were better than being dumped. For one more year we struggled with truths, lies, broken promises, hopes and reality. Fred had little qualities which could be applied toward building a relationship, any relationship. Years later I understood that, too. At that time I just held on to something which was never there and lost something which I never had. It was hard to let go of him and the pain that we manufactured together. When he was gone at last, the pain went away with him. There was an emotional echo in place of it. I didn't know what to do with the empty space, except to fill it with something else. I tortured myself with the memories of our experiences and wondered: 'What if I did...this, that or the next thing?

I decided to sell my house and return to New York City. I went to see Carla again and held on to her tight. I used her as my shelter against the world.

"Carla, my nightmares are back. I am so tired, you cannot know. I'm actually trying to sleep sitting up, hoping the dreams won't come that way." I confessed to her one day.

"When God sees that you have grown strong enough to face your nightmares, he will reveal them to you. Until then just pray for peace, Sugar, just pray to God for peace." She pulled my head onto her chest and caressed my hair.

In 1977 I became a US citizen and changed my legal name. All of my name. I wanted to hide behind a new identity. New name, new location, new life. Old me. I wanted nothing to do with anyone from my past. I didn't want to be found, bothered, looked up, surprised or the likes.

"You are your own past, Sugar," said Carla. "As long as you are you, all of your pasts are with you, no matter what name you call yourself by." She was right. "What you must do is, find out where you are going, look back into your past, understand the lessons in it, then turn around and use those lessons in your today and tomorrows." She kept petting my hair.

"I don't know how to do that. I don't really understand what you are talking about." I said to her with all honesty.

"You will, Sugar. You will." Carla seldom gave me advise to follow. She just loved me for every moment, every emotion, every thought, every feeling. She innately knew that I will find my own self someday, when I was good and ready to know who I really was and not deny it or try to color it. She patiently waited with me and accepted the me, I someday will also learn to accept.

Chapter 5

Buried but Not Gone

In 1978 my father passed away and I made the decision to go home and be present at his funeral.

I was scared, not knowing what the government would do to me but I went anyway. Kelly was ten years old and I was leaving her with a current boyfriend. It was late in October, cloudy and gray on the outside, cloudy and gray inside of me as well. Emotions, emotions, emotions. Old memories, forgotten faces, unanswered questions.

I left as a seventeen and a half year old massed up, fat, academic genius. I then was a thirty one year old massed up, skinny, interior designer with a beautiful daughter and a successful business. On the outside I've changed. In the inside? There I've changed also. I got worse. My mind stayed busy all through the flight.

Thirteen years brought my brother from twelve to twenty five years of age and I didn't recognize him at the airport. My mother, dressed in black looked more like my grandmother should have looked. My grandmother was the angel I always knew her to be. My mother cried and agonized in dramatic outbursts for the man who had also abused her physically, mentally, emotionally, spiritually and more. She missed him. She complained because I showed no signs of emotions, the likes she did. I was angry with her.

I was angry with my father for dying before I had a chance to show him that yes, I am somebody! I was angry with him for dying before I could confront him. Confront him with what? I didn't know. I hated him for not loving me and hoped that for a moment, for just a fleeting moment he thought of me before he died, that he felt some love for me. I went to see his open casket and in English, so no one would understand me, I told him all those thoughts. After the funeral, the family and friends got together and took inventory of the dead man's virtues and values. When my turn came up, all I could say was:

"I remember a completely different man." My mother began to cry again and I got up and walked out of the room. No regrets.

That night was a continuum of nightmares, the worse possible ones I had ever had! Still, I couldn't remember it as I bolted up in bed. I was exhausted. The last day of my visit I spent with my grandmother.

"My little sparrow," she said. She was ninety years old and looked and moved better than my mother who was only fifty eight. Grandma and I did not talk much. Mostly we sat in the same kitchen of the same house I grew up in, next to each other, on the same bed she shared with my grandfather since she married him at the age of thirteen. She laid me across her lap and brushed my hair with her crippled, arthritis pained fingers. Her sky blue eyes were filled with love and understanding and the clarity of deep vision beyond my comprehension. When I was with her I had no thoughts, only feelings. Feelings of peace and love, motionless serenity suspended somewhere far beyond gravity and conscious awareness. With grandmother I just was: perfect, innocent, sinless.   A newborn child, undaunted.

"You were my favorite," said she "you will always be. No matter how far you go, I am always with you. I'll be with you throughout your life. Trust in that. Trust in me. You will be happy someday but not for a while."

"But I am already happy, Grandma." I lied to her shamelessly.

"Hm. You may convince yourself of that but not this old crow. You have not, not yet been happy. Sure, there had been times in your life, when you were glad about this or that. Sure. But happy? No, little sparrow, you had not been happy. But you will be. And then, then you will remember me." She seemed to talk to the air rather than to me.

"Oh, Grandma, I think about you all the time! All the time!" I was assuring my angel.

"Yes. But remember? You don't remember me, yet." I had no idea what she was talking about. It didn't matter. There we were, together again and she was loving me. She loved me.

"Don't forget the wild herbs and oils we use to gather and press together. You were the only one of the flock who ever cared about the herbs and oils, you know? She reminded me of my early childhood, the walks we took hand in hand in the woods, her herb pantry and the bottles of oils and vinegars. Pictures formed in my mind and I smiled. She looked down at me and smiled herself. She had not one wrinkle on her face nor did she have a single tooth left in her mouth. Her skin was pink and smooth and flawless. Her eyes sparkled and could have won over any star in the sky. She lifted my spirit to limitless heights and mended and sheltered my broken soul, lovingly caressing my body. My grandmother. My Angel. I never saw her after that. She peacefully transited in her sleep, two years later.

Returning home, to the US was both hard and easy. I wanted to stay and be protected but I was ready to leave, knowing that there is love for me in this world. Most of our lives we all are looking for love in all the wrong places, overlooking or not even recognizing true love because it is not radiating from a body where our expectations lay.
I still didn't understand but was at the edge of sensing what love may be about.

Looking for love in all the wrong places.
Looking for God in all the wrong places.

1981. My world was an illusion and friends kept me safe in that seemingly painless world.

1982. Pictured at a meeting with some of the most important women of the islands.

Chapter 6

From Coast to Coast

Trouble broke loose as soon as I arrived at Kennedy Airport. The current boyfriend, with whom I was in a relationship and who was caring for my daughter during my travel, met me with an attitude and doubts of my whereabouts. He must have been waiting for me in the airport's bar for hours, because he was pretty well sauced by the time I landed. He staggered down the corridor with me to luggage claim, refusing to say a word. He didn't help with the suitcases and refused to let me drive home. He gave me a few nasty looks as he was drove, zigzagging from lanc to lane. I kept quiet. When we finally arrived at home he parked the car in the driveway and with the engine still running, said:

"So, where have you been, thrill seeker?"

"What do you mean, where had I been? I was in Europe, attending my father's funeral. You dropped off at the airport, remember?" I was being soft spoken and cautious. I had no idea what his problems were.

"Couldn't you have called? Don't they have a damn phone in that damn country that you could've call on?" He was decidedly drunk and mad about something.

"Yes, there are phones there but calling is not as easy as you would think. My family does not have a telephone and I would've had to try to call you from the Post Office. I had no time or opportunity to call anyone. I was at a hysterical funeral!" My patience was thin. I was tired and jet-lagged, rapidly growing irritated.

"What is your problem with me, anyway? Did anything go wrong while I was gone?" I finally asked him.

"You know, you're somethin' else," he hissed at me. "You dump your kid with me so you can go off and party, you bitch!"

"I wasn't partying!" I yelled back at him really loud, defending myself. "Would you tell me what the hell happened?" I lost my cool and was screaming at him.

"Your boyfriend Ed called, looking for you that's what! Said he called you before and you talked. He even asked you out!"

"Is that all?" I was calmer.

"Isn't it enough?" he yelled again. I almost laughed out loud, but didn't.

"First of all it's Fred, not Ed. If Fred called here looking for me while I was in Europe, I could not have been with him, could I? So, cool off, will you? Yes, Fred did call me at home, on my phone, probably twice in the last year or so. Yes, I did talk with him. I had no reason no to. Yes, Fred did ask me to meet him each time he called and no, I did not accept his invitation. And yes, I did ask him each time not to call me again. If he did, I can't help it. My phone number is a listed business number and I am not changing it. Sorry." I was done with the explanation.

It was the beginning of the end of that relationship. Rob became insanely jealous, possessive and demanding. He began calling me ten, even more times each day. He insisted on knowing my daily plans When I had a luncheon appointment he would show up in the same restaurant and watch me from a different table. He drank and got drunk daily. He went to his office later and later each day and after a few weeks he didn't go at all. He intimidated me every way he could. He decided to sit and stay in my office and listen to my telephone conversations. He began answering my phone and screen my calls. When I objected he accused me of hiding things from him. We argued and verbally abused each other. I heard Kelly cry at nights as she spent more and more time alone in her room. She withdrew from me and her friends.

I tolerated all of that until the first of February, 1979. On that night we had a violent argument and I made the decision to leave. Not just the relationship but the entire East Coast. I was drifting from one abuse to another for the past thirteen years of my American life. I had had it.

In the morning of February second 1979 I closed down my interior design business and all business accounts and obligations connected with it. I called Kelly's school and removed her from it. I packed my clothes, Kelly's clothes and stuffed animals, called a taxi and headed for Newark Airport. In the terminal, I stopped at the TWA ticket counter and asked the agent for the next available flight to the farthest US destination possible. Forty five minutes later Kelly, the stuffed toys and I boarded a jet heading for LA.

On the plane I got drunk. Kelly kept assuring me that everything will be O.K. We will be O.K. She promised to take care of me. We both cried, filled with relief and fear and every other old emotion. All we had was each other. Through the hopes and failures, the riches and poor, the angers, the shouts, through it all at each end and each beginning we had one another.

"I'll try to be a better mom, I promise you. I don't know how, but I'll try." I hugged my daughter close to me. I didn't know how to comfort her. I needed her to comfort me.

At LA Airport, I called a friend who worked in the same terminal we landed in. In fact, I could see him talking to me as I stood in the phone booth across the terminal.

"Kelly and I are just across from your window." I said to him. "Turn around and you'll see us." I waved to him as Kelly was running across the terminal toward him.

David and I had been wonderful and comforting friends to each other for a long time. Many years earlier I worked for him in Elizabeth, New Jersey. He had lost his little daughter, when she was five years old and the stress and grief had later caused his marriage to break up. He moved to California to start a new life for himself and we stayed in touch through phone calls and letters. We remained friends and friends alone, though years after my own arrival to California, on one of his own drunken nights he called and asked me to marry him. If he remembered such a proposal the next morning or not, I'm not aware of it. Only a few days after that call I left the country.

But for now, I was waving to my friend and Kelly ran across the terminal to greet him. It was wonderful to be with this friend again, even if it lasted only a short while. From David's apartment I called another friend, Doris who lived in San Diego. At the end of the week David drove us and left us in San Diego. We were homeless again, but we had good friends.

It took me a month to get situated, find a place to live, place Kelly in school and secure a job. I stretched my savings as far as it would stretch. All we had was winter clothes and stuffed animals. We had to start all over again. California was expensive and I produced little income compared to what I was used to producing. Once again, we struggled. Kelly became difficult, not understanding our situation and why we lived so poorly. I became depressed again, my nightmares returning. I worked at nights as a cocktail waitress and it meant alcohol. Lots of alcohol. Available alcohol. Customers offered and bought and I accepted and drank. I got drunk every day. the neighbors upstairs watched Kelly while I worked and she slept with them, so she didn't really see me in the condition I sometimes arrived in after work. I started to stock alcohol at home. I spent a lot of money on booze I couldn't afford, though I didn't have any parties at our apartment.

One day I noticed that there was a lot less liquor in my cabinet than should have been. 'Did I really drink that much?' I asked myself. Then I started to wonder if Kelly might be drinking, too. My suspicions were confirmed on one evening when I came home early from work, having a high fever and a head cold. She was entertaining some new friends with popcorn and brandy! Kelly was ten years old, the others, two boys and two girls, around twelve and thirteen. I didn't know what to do, so I told the four kids to leave immediately and scared as they were, they left. I looked at Kelly and she looked back at me defiantly with sparks in her eyes. I got angry. I raised my hand and slapped her across her face and hit her. It was not the first time I raised my hand to her, but it was the first time I gave her a beating. The first of many in the following three years.

I didn't consciously realize then that I had become my own father. I didn't realize many, many things, including how ill I was and the word *dysfunction* was foreign to me, even though dysfunction was all I had ever learned, known, practiced and passed on. Dysfunction was all that I could recognize and associate with. Well functioning people were uncomfortable to me, they intimidated and often bored me.

So, on that evening I passed on a family tradition: child abuse. It put both of us in terror of a new kind. Kelly became more and more hateful each day and I became more and more angry, frustrated and controlling. I didn't know how to be a loving parent though I loved my daughter very much. We seeked counseling and talked and yelled for an hour each week for about two months. We made a lot of noise without progress. We didn't listen. I couldn't afford to pay for our sessions any longer, so against the advice of the counselor, we stopped going. Kelly and I grew apart. When I smelled cigarette smoke on her breath, I ignored it. I didn't know what to do for her. I didn't know what to do for me! She did exactly as I did. I smoked, she smoked. I drank, she drank. If I wanted her to change, I needed to set an example of change. I just couldn't do that. I kept my valium locked in the glove compartment of my car. I was hoping she didn't know about them.

Though I did not actually take a drink in front of Kelly, I did slur my words and bumped into furniture in front of her.

I'm sure she had heard me flush the toilette after vomiting, also. the nightmares went away and I thought I was cool and unnoticed, my secret safe as I kept on drinking hour after hour, day after day, weeks, months years. I thought I was pretty cool. After a while, I didn't even think about what I was doing. I just did the same things over and over again, out of habit. I had none of the old pain and that's all that mattered.

It didn't take very long to find myself in another relationship. As one would guess, we met in the bar I was working at. This relationship lasted eleven years, survived nine years of marriage and in 1991 ended in a divorce.

Adam was a twice divorced attorney with a teenage daughter of his own, who lived with him. He thought I was beautiful, funny, energetic and would make a wonderful possession. Needless to say, he also drank and as before, I later found out that he also smoked pot with his *intellectual equals*. I joined them once or twice but really did not care much for the stuff. In the back of my mind I was still afraid of doing anything that was against the law, in fear of being deported, even though I had long before earned my citizenship. Drinking and valium were different. They were legal!

As the relationship continued, friends, both his and mine, encouraged us to make a deeper commitment. Adam had a lovely home about thirty miles Southeast of San Diego and by August of 1979 Kelly and I moved in with Adam and his teenage daughter, Kim. We had become the *ideal family,* destined to be successful.

Our life was an illusion, a facade which we kept up for years at any cost! And we were good at it, for no one suspected the life we lived within the privacy of our walls.

The girls hated each other. They were jealous and possessive, unwilling to share the only parent they each had. Kim's mother had been heavily involved with cocaine and had been in and out of prison, a small detail I was not aware of until many months after we had already lived together. Kim hated her mother for being that way and hated me for being better than her mother was. Kelly defended me and hated everybody for being stuck with the job of my defender. Adam thought I was beautiful and I made him look good.

I was really deep into misery not knowing what to do. I spent most of my life not knowing what to do. Still, we kept on playing our selected parts for many months to come: arguing, defending, accusing, denying, pretending.

In 1980 I got very ill and had to have a complete hysterectomy and two months after that surgery I lost my voice completely and underwent another surgery on my vocal cords. Adam was forced to take charge of both girls, which, predictably turned out to be a disaster. Kim threaten to move in with her grandmother, which Adam could not allow for appearances' sake.

Later that year came a job opportunity for Adam which required a move to the South Pacific Islands of Palau. He flew to LA for the interview and having beaten out two hundred other applicants, he got the job as a Federal Public Defender.

Having lived in this country for fifteen years, I was about to leave it, because Adam wanted me to go with him. I wasn't sure. I struggled to get here, to get anywhere and now leave it? I'd set a condition for us to get married first. We decided to go through with it. Since Kim wanted to live with her grandmother already, Adam let her stay behind. She was fifteen years old. Kelly was coming with us. Even though we had very little idea of what to expect, she decided it was going to be perfect anywhere just as long as Kim was not there with her.

Chapter 7

Worlds Apart

Since I already crossed the sea once, both Adam and Kelly looked to me for guidance during our time of preparation for this enormous change. I faked security, radiated calmness and tranquillity while battled with my own internal termoiles. Once committed, all three of us stuck to it, stuck within it, stuck with our own illusions. On a few occasions, when I expressed my doubts to my friends I was quickly put straight by them:

"I can't believe you're even thinking about not going! What do you mean, you're not sure you want to marry Adam? Are you crazy? You two are perfect together. I envy you, you dummy!" Said a girlfriend at a party, only a couple of weeks before we were to leave.

"You'd be stupid not to marry him," said another.
I didn't want to seem stupid, so we got married in Hawaii on our way to Palau, to a new life. I looked good. I felt confused. Adam thought I was beautiful. Kelly was happy because we left Kim in California. With those basic emotions, qualities and pretenses we laid our foundations for another part of our lives.

If we expected something different we certainly got it, though I don't remember actually talking about our individual preconceived ideas. But different it was. More like primitive, after having lived in a four bedroom custom designed home with Spanish - tile lined swimming pool, Jacuzzi and romantic fire-pit to sip delicate wine by, nestled among graceful, cool shading eucalyptus trees in the best climate of the entire North America: San Diego.

What we got was tropics. Tropics with 88°F and 88% humidity for twenty four hours a day, twelve hours of which was blasting sun and exactly twelve hours of it was pitch dark. No tradewinds, only a daily monsoon that drenched us each day between 12:15 and 12:30 PM as if the heavens broke loose. Rainwater ran like a river, seeking the ocean and when the sun emerged again, humidity rose to its maximum capacity and every bit of clothing stuck to all bodies and hung in there like a scare- crow's would after a storm. Make up melted on my face and mascara made black tracks downward on my cheeks. My hair hung in clumps like Raggedy Ann's and I didn't feel so beautiful.

The natives waged bets on how long I would stay and the most I was given was two weeks.

I lived there for over four years and loved every moment of every day in those years. Even the ones I didn't like. I learned to forget and I learned to learn even though I was not consciously aware of all those lessons at that time.

My marriage was not made in heaven. Even though we took our wows in *paradise*, it was far from it. We left everything behind to start anew except our dysfunctions. The native children hated Kelly and she attempted suicide on my valiums. I flushed them down the toilet and gave them up for life.

About a year after our arrival, Adam was appointed to the bench thus became the youngest Federal Justice of the Peace to that date. It was in 1981. I met some of the most important dignitaries from all over the Pacific and Asia. We wined and dined with them. We partied with the socially and politically correct from senators to congressmen, ministers to the honored Queen, High Chief, President and Vice President. We traveled to wonderful, exotic places around the world like: Singapore; Malaysia, where I climbed the Batu caves; Bali, where I became mesmerized by the gentleness of Hinduism; Thailand, where I floated on a bamboo raft as my hotel room over the River Kwai and my dinner was prepared from my own choice of chicken; in the Philippines I climbed the ancient rice terraces built by the Ifugaos and Igorots more than two thousand years ago; in Hong Kong I watched the most spectacular fireworks on

162

New Year's Eve; in China I was served and eleven course dinner, one course more delicious than the other; in Japan I saw Mount Aso go pooff and I boiled eggs at the hot springs of Bepu. I imagined the nuclear horrors of Nagasaki and Hiroshima as I walked through the museums and monuments of those cities; in Macau I saw some of the worlds most beautiful silk flowers ever made; Jakarta showed me poverty which I did not imagine could exist. I appreciated them all! Every whim of my ego was fulfilled.

The president of Palau asked me to open the Inaugural Ball with him because his Saturday Adventist wife was not allowed to dance. He asked me! I accepted and I danced. My pictures, dancing with the President were on the front page of most newspapers throughout the Pacific and Asia. I was beautiful, said the crowd. I was a *princess*, I had it all. No kingdom or crown, but certainly a lot of hoopla. Adam was doing well and I was looking good. I was unhappy.

I took an interest in the local culture and history and started to spend more and more time with the native people. I was given permission to attend special events and celebrations where non-natives or non-relatives were not allowed before. I was hungry for something, anything they could feed to me. This hunger was roaring somewhere deep inside of me, somewhere in the very core of my heart. I watched and I observed and I absorbed.

Adam thought I was getting too involved with the people and said so and he said it often. I tried to explain to him how much I was learning and how very little I knew, still. He believed that his *position* required more detachment. I believed that mine required less. We argued in privacy, smiled in public. We were looking good. I was unhappy.

Kelly threatened to run away from home. I gave her permission. I figured that an island which is only one mile wide and four miles long is only able to provide her with a few options. When she returned six hours later, she brought home with her a white puppy. It was probably the ugliest little puppy I ever laid eyes on but she loved that dog with rare devotion, unconditionally. Kelly was a physically stunning child and now a teenager of rare beauty. But her true beauty came through the love she showered onto that dog. It was a quality in her that I never noticed before. One of many, many beautiful qualities she still, as a grown woman possesses today.

After her running away from home a new kind of stress took shape. I didn't know what name it hid behind, I just knew that there it was. Seemingly I had everything: a husband with a high, rare position, a stunningly beautiful daughter, respect and admiration of people from all walks of life, all corners of the world. Sill, I was unhappy. My nightmares returned, I couldn't sleep. When I finally fell asleep it was near morning and I was tired. I returned to heavy drinking at nights so that I could sleep. I got drunk every night I know it, though I did it quietly.

Once at a party, I watched people as they were drinking, putting down one drink after another and I saw how different they were from me. Just like at my graduation party years before, they seemed to loosen up, became more relaxed and seemed to have fun, laughing and joking with each another. I realized then that I never felt like that. I never had fun when I drank. I always drank to make some pain go away. I drank to get drunk so I wouldn't hurt. Yet, among those people not one of them looked to me as though they were in any kind of pain. I envied them for being able to have fun. I didn't drink any alcohol up to that point yet, still I was not having fun. Sober or drunk, I didn't know what it felt like to have fun. Suddenly, the pain deep inside of me fired up. I walked to the bar and claimed my share of the *fun.*

I had open access to most government buildings and offices and I frequently made my rounds, creating and collecting friends wherever I went. People were wonderful to me and I had grown to respect and love them individually and collectively. My best friend was the wife of the Vice President. We lived only a few houses apart on the same street and she often *ran away from home* to spend time with me. She was a huge woman with a heart of a giant and in my own estimation she would have made the best World Peace Ambassador. I loved her perhaps more than she loved herself, because even though she had a bad heart, she continually smoked, drank, ate the worse possible foods the land had to offer and she chewed the famous and traditionally accepted Beetle Nut, which is an adjustable strength narcotic depending on the combination of the ingredients of Queen palm nut, boiled and crushed lime powder rolled up into a pepper leaf and then chewed, producing a feeling of tranquillity and a scary, bright red liquid/saliva mixture which the chewer spits out (anywhere within spit distance). It also causes gum and tooth deterioration and an ugly smile. After a while I got used to seeing it as part of the culture.

It also is very much part of the native culture to share or at least offer whatever a person has and on a single occasion I tried this Beetle Nut thing. I didn't like it and in good humor I was laughed at for my expression of the drug. It tasted foul though somewhat sweet. It released its effect rather quickly which also scared me. I mused at how openly most adults and even some children chewed the thing, knowing it's effect. Still, it was cultural and ancient tradition.

During the second year of my life in Palau, the second lady and I along with about ten or so other woman, mostly wives of politicians, founded a non-profit organization to provide much needed aid to the native handicapped children. I became a national hero and received some wonderful recognition, one of which was a congressional honor all of my own, aside from my husband's important position. Adam's ego flared in jealously as he rained on my parade. We truly did not understand or support each other. Without my civic involvement all I had was the house which I kept immaculately clean and needed no more than a half hour each day to maintain. The rest of the time I could measure the size of cockroaches that grew as large as sparrows or I could play with geckoes and lizards. Or I could count the giant African snails slithering across my front yard. I read all the romance novels I could to further depress myself because my own marriage was not getting any more fulfilling. My nightmares kept me awake and tired. I needed the activity to physically and mentally exhaust myself so I could just go to sleep at nights.

One of the local senators who befriended both of us, made a comment one day:

"Are you all right, Manonne? I noticed that lately you look tired." He sounded concerned.

"Oh, I haven't been sleeping well lately and I have a hard time staying awake during the day." I told him. "I have a hard time getting my energy together, that's all." We didn't say anything else about it. He smiled and gave me a hug. I went home. Less than an hour later there was a knock on our door and when I opened it, there stood my senator friend with a small pouch in his hand and a big smile on his face.

"I brought something to cheer you up," he said.

""Come on in." I invited him just as I had done many times before.

"What'd you got?" I asked.

"Let's sit down." He sat down at the kitchen table, placing and opening his pouch.

"It is not good seeing you like this. You are not yourself anymore. I bring to you something that will make you feel much better in no time at all. No problem, O.K.?"
Our senator friend introduced me to and got me hooked on cocaine for the following eight years. He supplied me with the stuff non-stop and I probably had the very best and purest available anywhere. He came to our house more and more frequently, usually when he was sure that Adam was in trial. He told me how beautiful and wonderful I was and how much he loved me. He said that if anything should happen between me and Adam, he'd be there for me, he'll make me

166

his wife and take care of me and Kelly. He told me that he knew how unhappy I was and not to be afraid because he was there to love me. He told me all that stuff over and over again, all through to the last day of my stay in Palau. We never had an affair. He hugged and kissed me on my forehead and brought me my coke. Part of me believed him, but a larger part of me needed him. He made my nightmares go away. I was able to cut back on my alcohol use without missing it or craving it. I didn't know that I was getting hooked on some very serious stuff. I don't know if I cared. All I cared about was not to feel that pain.

My relationship with Kelly surprisingly improved.
I removed her from school to start her on correspondence studies through the University of Nebraska with a private tutor. She was doing very well. Her papers were returned with high grades and we spent lots of time together, getting along.

Adam was busy judging people, I was busy defending them, learning from them, trying to live as simple as they did. Both our names made the newspapers, almost on the weekly basis. We each were doing our own thing. Growing. Growing apart.

In the summer of 1984 Adam wanted to go to Europe on our vacation. We few to Hong Kong and on to Italy. Rome, Florence, Venice, up north to Switzerland, Austria and into Hungary where my family was living. At was the first time that Kelly met the only family she had besides me.

My brother was married with a newborn son of their own. We stayed at my mother's house, the same house I grew up in. Memories returned and I felt uncomfortable. For the first few nights I couldn't fall asleep at all. Anxiety and panic attacks overwhelmed me to a point where I had to spend most of the time outdoors. One morning, in a half sleep I heard loud voices from the kitchen. My mother and my brother were fighting over something. At first, I thought that Kelly may have done something to agitate one of them but as I kept listening I found out differently.

"I told you before and now I am telling you for the last time. If you even as much as think about giving that child any alcohol, you are not going to see us again! Do you understand what I am saying, Mama? Don't even think about it because you will lose all of us, like you lost my sister!" My brother yelled at the top of his lungs.

"Come on Son, what's the matter with you? Why are you making such a big deal? All I did was rubbed a tiny bit of brandy over his gums. He's teething Son, can't you see it hurts his little gums?" My mother explained.

"Listen to me, Mama. You had done this to me, you had done this to Baba. We both got hooked on alcohol, just like you did. I am not going to allow you to do the same thing to my son! You are not going to turn my son into another family drunk! I'm not gonna let you, do you understand me?" My brother was yelling.

"What do you mean you not gonna let me! I'm your mother, you can't boss me around like that, you can't tell me what to do!" My mother yelled back at him.

"I know who you are. Do you know who I am? I am a grown man! I am the father of that little boy. He is my child not yours and I will make decisions about what anybody can or cannot do for him! Do you understand me? If he is teething, he is teething. All babies go through teething. He's not the only one. But not all babies get brandy because of it. Teething is natural, Mama. He can deal with it. All other babies learn to deal with it without getting drunk. Now, I wasn't just threatening you before. If I ever catch you giving my son any booze again, that will be the last time you will ever see us. I mean it!"

I was standing inside the front porch listening and watching them through the window. My brother lifted the baby out of the stroller, got into his car and took off steaming angry. Neither of them had seen me, I was sure of that. I walked back to the sitting room and sat down with a

168

thousand thoughts and memories of my own. Interestingly enough, I wasn't sure which of them were right. I was confused. Part of me agreed with my brother: how could she give booze to a little baby? Part of me agreed with my mother: I've been treated the same way, so what's the big deal? Then it dawned on me: 'She did do the same thing with me! Could it be the reason why I am the way I am?' Consciously, I had nothing to hold onto but inside of me things were stirring and battling. I didn't know how to deal with my new discomfort. I didn't understand my discomfort, so I went to the bedroom, lay down on the bed and decided to take a nap. (When all else fails, hide!)

I felt restless for the rest of our vacation. I spent seemingly the longest three weeks of my life during that vacation. I am grateful for the time and for overhearing the experience between my mother and my brother. The memory of it was very helpful later on as my healing and letting-go process evolved.

After we returned to the island Adam and I made the decision to enter Kelly into a regular US school system for her senior year. It meant a return to mainland USA, and in May of 1985 Kelly and I flew to San Diego, picked up the few belongings which we left behind in storage, bought my wonderful T'bird and drove to one of the most beautiful little towns in North Idaho called: Coeur d'Alene, where we settled as our new home. Adam came to help us settle in, but was soon returning to his judgeship which was a life time appointment for him.

Before his return, Adam purchased a small gift store for me, so I'll have something to *entertain* myself with while he was making decisions about people's freedom and Kelly was taking in the virtues and values of senior year high school. Another start.

Adam called every week and wrote beautiful words into letters, such as I never heard him say to me in person. Kelly went to school, each day adjusting to a culture she left behind when she was only eleven years old. She was then sixteen. I was pouring all of my energy into running a business which I knew nothing about. It was stressful for all of us. Soon though, we all found our own pace and became more comfortable in our new roles.

Kelly joined the community theater. She was talented and she sparkled. She made friends. I created not only income but profit through my new, small business which was supposed to had been only entertainment for me. The local newspaper took an active interest in my *island life* and released articles on me which perked public curiosity and business profits. I was content. I was busy.

My senator friend wrote, still assuring me of my safe future. Adam called, complaining. He was lonely. When he came home for a visit, we didn't know what to say to each other. He examined the books and was shocked at how well I did with the business. He purchased another store (a corner drug store with a pharmacy), then an office building, then another building and finally resigned form his judgeship and came home permanently.

He came home to take control of his businesses and his possessions, including me and Kelly. I was reluctant to let go of what I thought I built. We, the three of us found ourselves once again in the old power struggle of wanting to control each other. I wanted to hear Adam's praises of how well I conducted our business in his absence. It never came. Instead, he was jealous of my accomplishments and determined to outdo me. When he couldn't, he began verbally pounding on me until I felt like a shredded rag. I didn't understand any of it. I left the management of the businesses and filled with resentment and utter disappointment, stayed at home seeking comfort in old friends. My bottles and my powders. I didn't care about the outside world anymore.

Kelly ran away from home again and for an entire month we had no idea where she could be. Each time the phone rang I panicked, expecting the worse news. After a month that news came. A hospital, forty five miles away called, where they just finished pumping her stomach to remove the drugs she was hoping to overdose on. I dressed frantically to go and be with her and as I was about to run out the door Adam called after me:

"I hope you realize that she can't just waltz back into this house and be forgiven. I hope you know that she can't come back and live with us!" He was speaking quietly and with meaning.

"No, I didn't know, I didn't even think about that." I answered him. "She's my daughter and she'll be where I'm at. If she can't be here, I can't be here. I gotta go now." I shut the door behind me and drove the forty five miles in the middle of the night to see my pained and confused child. All along the way a single thought kept repeating in me over and over again: 'like mother, like daughter - like mother, like daughter'. My little girl was growing up to be like me. For the first time in my life I was overran by the heaviest burden of guilt, almost unbearable to carry.

Kelly lay in a tiny bed of a tiny room, all bruised, pale and weak.

"I'm sorry Mama," was all she had the strength to whisper. Then her eyes filled with tears and she closed her lids as those tears ran down her sunken cheeks and she kept on crying and crying, silently, to herself.

"I love you. Angel, I love you very much." I was trying to assure her. I took her into my arms and held her, rocking her weak little body way past the time she fell into a natural sleep. She was seventeen years old and probably hurting from the events of her past just as I was pained by something in my past. Deep, unexplainable pain that came without notice, whenever it chose to. I wanted so much to tell her that I understood but I didn't know how to say it. I didn't know what it was that I understood. Maybe it was just the pain. I understood pain. Like mother, like daughter.

Kelly did not get to come home to live with us. She moved in with a friend, instead. Adam was relieved. Kelly made no secret about her emotions toward Adam.
I understood and secretly joined her in her feelings.

I could go on and on detailing the various workouts I gave to my developing dysfunction. Just as my mother had ignored my needs for emotional development, I did likewise with Kelly. I didn't know what else to pass onto her, other than what I had learned. Even though I sensed that something, everything was wrong, I had no idea how to undo it. No one ever taught me to.

I couldn't teach or give what I didn't have.

Staying at home gave me an opportunity not only to drink and use but paint. Ten years earlier when I was studying interior design, I discovered that I had a keen eye for color, form and dimension. I produced a limited number of canvases then which I quickly sold. Until now I didn't even think about painting, no less painting again. But, out of the blue the thought came and I yielded.

I used oils which have a distinct odor and Adam detected it as soon as he entered the house. I did not allow him to see what I was painting, but promised him that he'll be the first to see the final picture. True to my word, when I felt that the painting was done I revealed my creation to him. It was a very large canvas, showing a woman in a beautiful white dress, holding an open parasol, looking out to the ocean. I was proud of my painting. Adam, on the other hand could only say:

"So what else can you do that you didn't tell me about, yet?"

When the painting was dry and framed I sold the it to a Canadian attorney, who later became a collector of my works. Adam couldn't feel any joy for me. If he did, he didn't share it with me. I kept on painting, drinking and using all in the privacy of my home, secretly. I sold my paintings easily and quickly and when we purchased an antique and art gallery I displayed and marketed my work in it.

Kelly didn't return home and I never stopped feeling guilty about it. Adam and I drifted farther and farther away, until the gap became too wide and deep. There was no turning back. The final blow came when Kelly announced that she was pregnant and was about to be married to the father of her baby. I knew it was not going to be the answer but I encouraged her to go ahead with their plans, anyway. We held the wedding ceremony in our house, to Adam's total displeasure.

The marriage didn't make it, but they collaborated in the production of a sweet, healthy and perfectly angelic little boy -- Jason. I have to give the kids, now parents, a lot of credit. They did try to function as best they could. But neither of them had a stable, solid emotional foundation no matter how hard I wished otherwise.

My own marriage was beyond repair and neither of us tried anymore. I did the best I could at hiding and pretending, keeping alive the illusion of being the perfect social couple. How in the world did we manage to hide behind our facade and keep up appearances, I do not know. By the spring of 1989 I was deep into the white powder and back at the bottom of the bottle. Adam bought me expensive cognacs for my birthday and other occasions, only to watch me get drunk and cynically label me an alcoholic. I didn't care. By then I was empty of all emotions and hopelessness and helplessness were my constant states of mind. I no longer wanted to be near Adam. I didn't want to hear his voice, smell his scent or sense his touch. I didn't want to see him. My hate for men returned along with the nightmares filled with the terrifying demons. I still could not remember them upon awakening. They became worse and worse, more frequent and more and more powerful. I had terrible sensations of falling through my mattress, far, far down, being sucked into a deep, black bottomless pit. I had to hold onto the edge of my mattress to stop myself from falling. I had even tore holes into it as I dug in with my nails, holding on. I truly wanted to die more often than not.

Adam led me to believe that people hated me because I was a drunk, so I felt isolated, abandoned, cast aside like a pile of dirt.

On the day of her divorce, Kelly came back with my grandson, Jason and stayed for three months, until she was able pull her own broken life together and get a small place for herself and the baby. I watched and thought: 'Like mother, like daughter.' It was good to have her there again but she seldom stayed with me, trying real hard to get her own little life into some kind of order. Soon after they moved out I became more and more depressed. When I wasn't depressed I was unreasonably euphoric and my moods were swinging like a pendulum: up and down. Sinking or flying. Never standing still, never peaceful. I lost weight and interest in life. I lost interest in painting. All I did was used and drank and go out to buy more stuff to use and drink.

By May 16, 1989 I created a monster. I turned a beautiful woman into an alcoholic junky, only I was still not aware of it. The awareness came the very next morning when, as I was wasting my body and my mind under the dining room table and was forced to listen to a story about some dirty bird called phoenix, God once again sent his golden light into me and caused me to make my own transformation.

How could I put into words what it feels like to feel as I do now? Perhaps I could speak it but not write it. Perhaps I could say only that you must, your own self experience it since this feeling is seeded in my heart not in my mind. I could say to you that this feeling is the richest of all feelings and it is limitless because the more I share it the more I have to give it all over again. And I share this feeling with you through each hug and smile and thought I now have and I share it with you through each word written on the pages of this book and I will never get tired of sharing it. And I say to you that whatever I have done or whatever you have done does not matter. What matters is what we do with those experiences and how soon can we undo the results by not repeating them.   Because you see, we can undo them. When I fall down, I undo my fall by getting up. When I have a negative thought I can undo that thought by replacing it with a positive one. We can reverse all things by thinking, saying and doing the opposite.

You don't believe me? Than change your mind and you will!

One fear I overcame was my fear of water.
I learned to scuba dive.

Part III

Chapter 1

Dawning...

I am well now. Physically, emotionally, mentally and spiritually. Today, as I teach (and sometimes preach) the virtues of healing and transformation, the one thing I keep hearing repeatedly is:

"It's a lot easier said than done!"

Oh, how true it is! For some people. Not for *us*!

It took me *one moment*! And the next moment after that and the next one after that. Often a day, even an hour was much too long. One moment at a time. One step at a time. One thought at a time. The very first thing I had to do was, to somehow unlearn the things I already knew. Honestly! I figured out that I said and did things which I had learned from different people at different times in my life, and since my life had not been so terrific in the past, I must not have learned and remembered things very well, so why not forget the whole thing and start over again? Starting over was not new to me, anyway!

I started to doubt all the things that I had been taught. I didn't really have any particular idea or thought to start with, I just let my mind pick whatever it wanted and I went along with it. I figured, there was plenty wrong going on inside that mind of mine to be busy with for quite some time! I started to pay attention to small things - simple words - at first. It took hours and I was fascinated by it. I realized that things are not always what they seem to be! A miserable, cold winter day is really not bad at all.   It supposed to be miserable and cold! The more time I spent on seeing differently the more I understood myself.

I began to understand that my anger was a reaction to something or someone I felt insecure about. It was my ego's struggle to control. Usually something or someone it had no business controlling to begin with! The more I learned to understand about myself, the less my family and friends understood me. It was O.K., though.

In situations when I would get a really bad feeling usually do to other people's opinions, I would *still patiently listen. After they were done, I would thank them for their thoughts and I'd smile. Then I would quietly walk away! A behavior totally opposite to what I did before, when I argued and fought and yelled and brought myself into a state of frenzy and complete exhaustion. Moment by moment I taught myself to be accepting, yet not settling. To be assertive, yet not rude. To be firm, yet not controlling. To be determined, yet not be stubborn. To be committed, yet not be rigid and so on. I had learned to listen without allowing myself to be affected by the things I was hearing.*

I created a comfort zone for myself and I *set boundaries around that comfort zone. Not to lock myself in, rather to block danger and confusion out. Those boundary lines (rules) kept me safe and secure within as I grew stronger. Finally, I invented a word game for myself. Even today I use this little game as a*
reminder that there are always choices.

Remembering some of my science studies, I knew that everything has a positive and negative aspect to itself. There is a positive and negative side to things, including words, which are nothing more than the noises of our thoughts flowing through intellectually comprehensible

178

patterns of vibrations! (Wow!) Using this very simple formula, I looked at some negative words which I frequently heard or used myself and searched for all possible words of their positive side.

For example:

        bad - - - - - - good
        dark - - - - - -light
        restless - - -content
        scattered - united, etc.

It was self training in search of options, to think more positively in a general sense. As I continued growing into this new habit, (it did take a little while to discipline myself) I expended this game into thought patters.

For instance:

        boundary - -became safety zone
        rule - - - - - - a discipline
        struggle - - -a chance to resolve a puzzle
        problem - - -now was an opportunity for a new

challenge. *I refused to recognize problems . I still do not have any problems. What I have are ongoing lessons to grow and learn from to become the best that I can be.*

When I arrived at ego, I needed a lot more time to understand as best as I could. This is what I came up with:

Ego - my conscious awareness or conscious mind. A central point of all of my senses in charge of my decision making, my acting and reacting to everything and everyone outside of myself. My ego is my human intellect, my human understanding and awake self. It is the decision maker and cause of my physical and emotional states of being.

After ego, came the words: thought and feeling. I really needed to slow down and take my time to be clear and precise about those two.

As I understand we have *two different kinds of thought. One is, when we make a conscious effort, we invest some time to create ideas in. The other thoughts simply occur to us. One we consciously create, the other comes free of any of our conscious effort. A thought is happening in our mind - conscious or otherwise.*

A *feeling* was a little more complex and I am now going to dissect this word into *three different meanings* which we, in our lazy English language simply clump together. We express feelings such as: *happy, sad, angry, cold, thirsty, calm* and so on. As I clearly understand the differences of these various expressions today, I will attempt to clarify those differences as best as I can.

When we are: *cold, hungry, tired, achy, thirsty*, etc., we are not feeling but *physically sensing* something in *various parts of our body.* We are experiencing a *physical sensation*, not a feeling. These sensations are happening to us because something is lacking from the outside. As soon as we fill that lack with food, drink, warm clothing, etc., we no longer sense the physical sensation. We return to natural comfort. We no longer think about it. We are comfortable. We feel wonderful, at ease. So *a physical sensation is caused by something lacking from the outside, and is always negative.* Once the lack is removed we return to natural ease and balance. Let's say then that what we experience in our bodies are not feelings but *sensations* and they *are negative.*

Other types of expressions we call feelings are: *angry, sad, jealous, anxious, guilty, fearful, depressed,* etc. These feelings are called: *emotions.* All of these emotions are also happening to us because of some external cause by someone or something. These things are not really happening in our bodies, though we usually have a physical sensation along with the emotion. *An emotion occurs in our mind someplace.* As I began to spend more

and more time learning about myself, I came to understand that my *emotions were also greatly dependent on something or someone on the outside of myself.*
I became angry, because I didn't get what I expected from someone; I became anxious because I anticipated something to go wrong or I became jealous because I couldn't control someone to behave in a way I wanted them to behave.

I realized that most of my emotions also had everything to do with my reactions to the world around me, outside of me. When things were going my way, I was O.K. When things - be it real or imagined - were in order, I had no emotions. As long as I could control things around me, I felt good. When I began to sense some weakness in my control over the world outside of myself, some emotion flared up and I no longer felt so good. When I let go of my control of the world outside of myself, I started to feel better. I am now certain that *emotions are also negative.*

I also noticed that *not all of my emotions originated from the outside.* Some came from deep within me without notice, seemingly for no particular reason. They were powerful though, often much more powerful than the ones caused by my struggle for control. At first I didn't understand them but I was sure that no matter where they were coming from, they did not feel good, so *I firmly stand on all emotions being negative.*

Well, what about *feelings*? I know that there were moments here and there when I felt at least O.K. When everything was O.K. on the outside as well as on the inside, I felt pretty good, I thought. Still, what are these so called: good feelings? Well, there were times when I felt calm, even peaceful. *At these times of feeling good there was nothing that disturbed me. Nothing from the world around me, nothing from inside of me.* There was just a big nothing to interfere with what must have been occurring to me naturally. *Without emotions and physical sensations I was feeling good.* There was a part to me which kept me *feeling good naturally* when my body and my emotions were at ease. But where is this part? What do I call it? Some people refer to it is the *child within.* Science named it the *unconscious mind.* Others call it the *subconscious mind.* I call it *spirit.* It sounds naturally comfortable for me to call that part of me spirit.

My spirit has the ability to provide me with: peace, serenity, joy, love, freedom, etc. These are only some of the feelings that we have which are true feelings that we carry with us, we are made of as our eternal essence, our spirit selves. They do not require anything from the outside to be with us. A feeling is complete within its own self. A feeling is the invisible web of eternal life, woven of boundless joy, serenity, peace, tranquillity, love and freedom, among many other wonderful unnamed feelings. A feeling is created by God and is given into each of us as the sustaining component of who we are. A feeling requires no external stimuli to be whole. It is whole within its own life, it is life itself. It is connected to the rhythmic pulsation of the river of life, as a drop of water is connected to the entire body of waters wherever that water is located - be it an ocean, a brook, a raindrop or a tear. It is the connecting link to all other waves and vibrations of life. They are always there and I feel them just as soon as I let go of things and people from the outside and my emotions from the inside and wrap myself up in a soft, warm blanket of it. This spirit is also in charge of all other, naturally occurring activities inside and outside of me, which I do not consciously create or even think about. My spirit keeps me breathing, keeps my heart beat, makes my hair grow, replaces my worn out, even dead body cells, monitors the temperature of my immediate surroundings, plus does six trillion other things - per second! All that is taking place without the involvement of my conscious mind or ego.

Let me sum up what I have written so far:

My conscious mind is my ego, my intellect, the interpreter of the world around me. It is the decision maker in me. It sees and decides, judges, litigates, barters and argues. It creates havoc and confusion. It has a temper. It wants to control. It is the maker of my emotions. It thinks. It thinks it knows it all!

My spirit is my constantly awake, but silent self. It is the part of me that holds the eternal, universal knowledge which I brought with me to release to my human self, to my ego, to aid in its purification and assention into the world of my spirit. It is the master teacher in me as I now live my life.

My body is the mobile vehicle that takes my ego and my spirit from one place to another, hopefully with some purpose.

body - sensation - (matter) - negative
mind - ego - (conscious) - emotion - negative
spirit - self - (subconscious) - true feeling - positive

With those three parts put together I am a human being. Complete. Not perfect, but complete.

My body is tangible, it has visual substance. It feeds on measurable matter. It is measurable. It moves.

My mind is intangible, it has no visual substance. It feeds on perception, judgment, information, understanding and experience. It has a limited capacity to retain. It cannot be seen, though we have evolved in our scientific development to the ability to measure it. It thinks. It has the ability to travel. At times, it is all over the place.

My spirit is intangible, it has no visual substance and we have yet to evolve in our scientific development to measure it, but it is there, has been there since creation and will remain throughout creation. It is a connecting link in the chain of universal knowledge, the expression of the continual flow of universal love, life, harmony and balance, gushing through our entire being.
Body - Mind - Spirit.

So, how is it, that we feel bad?

What happens is, a struggle develops between my knowing spirit and my thinking mind. At first this struggle is silent and unnoticed, occurring someplace behind the scene much like a rehearsal does before the actual theater play. It's happening, but we are not aware of it. Over some time this struggle becomes more and more noticeable as our subconscious mind or spirit speaks up against the ego's inputs of un-truths, attempting to reveal the truth of knowledge. Some of the results of this internal struggle then reflects through either our body as a physical sensation, or in our mind as an emotion, most of the time, both. We begin to feel at unease. How does all that happen?

Earlier I stated that our spirit is knowledge, it knows and our ego is (part) or though, it thinks (it thinks it knows it all!). The ego operates as a receptor (computer keyboard or scanner) of things that are happening around me. It sees, hears, smells, tastes, interprets experiences and sends all that stuff into my subconscious mind for storage. Much like punching the keys on the keyboard of my computer. When I type in: 'I love you', it registers in the main brain (subconscious) is truth and accepts it without needing any correction. If I type in the same letters in a different order such as: 'I vleo uyo', the main brain of my computer will spit it out as incorrect information, not having

184

a clue as to what to do with it. The information I put in did not register (as truth). I can choose to ignore it even after several spell checks but it will keep on returning to my screen demanding to be corrected each time it has an opportunity to do so. Ultimately I will have to make the necessary corrections and put it to rest. Much the same with us.

All through the times when my ego perceived my *dysfunctional experiences as acceptable truths and sent those information to my memory bank as such, my spirit protested by sending messages back through my body as ill sensations and through my mind as emotions. I ignored them, because to my perceptive mind they seemed to be truths.*

The first question is: "What were those *dysfunctional* experiences?"

Any type of behavior which is not naturally comfortable to all living things involved in an experience is dysfunctional to one participant or the other, because it causes ill - ease. Consuming alcohol, drugs, receiving physical, emotional or psychological abuse, molestation or rape are all part of dysfunctional experiences.

The second question could be: "Why then, did I send those message as natural experiences if they were indeed, not?" My own understanding is that since the ego has no accumulated knowledge at birth, it simply perceives and accepts experiences as they come. As these experiences repeat over and over again, they become *accepted (habitual) patterns of function. They become 'truths', as far as the ego is concerned. In my practice, I refer to this phenomenon as: social and environmental hypnosis of infantile conditioning. The ego thinks that all that garbage is truth because those are the things that keep repeating and that is what it learns as truth. We cannot consciously learn the things we are not exposed to, we cannot send*

185

them to the memory bank for storage to be retrieved for use at a later time. We simply cannot consciously know what we didn't learn. We rely on the information that we perceive as truth, no matter how much our spirit tries to alert us.

Further more, these dysfunctional experiences are being repeated by those people around us whom we are frequently exposed to, rely on, people who supposed to love, protect and nurture us. People, who we supposed to trust unquestioningly. People, whom we do trust unquestioningly!

Instead of standing still silently without any conscious thought and allowing my all-knowing spirit to guide me onto the path of function, I chose to ignore my spirit, that all knowing vital part of me and continued to silence my internal screams. As the screams became louder and louder, I put more and more *stuff, which I knew would keep it quiet, into my body. More and more untruths, until the time came when there was no more room left to store any more lies in. I had to stop and listen to my spirit. I had to stop and listen to the truth.*

My own dysfunction was created by the combined efforts of my family's own inability to deal with life and the input of my ego. It is basically very simple. Each time the ego makes an inaccurate assessment or more clearly, lies to the spirit, the balance -feeling- inside of us is rocked like a - boat - a - float and we experience an imbalance through our emotions. This imbalance is fed back into our body and we experience a physical sensation as well. We receive two alert signals as warnings, still we do nothing about them. Why?

Because we don't know what to do! No one thought us! We made a mistake and there was no one else around to show us how to fix that mistake right after we'd done it. See how simple it is? Not yet? O.K.

Emotion. We used to call it a feeling but now we know that it is not. It is one of the results of our ego's interpretation of how it perceives the activities around itself. Emotion is the outcome or result of how our ego chooses - from millions of available choices - to judge, determine, understand, accept and finally react to any given experience. It is through selecting from the unlimited choices that the ego must learn all those things which our spirit essentially knows. The ego is our human component, it is here to learn the knowledge of our spirit and reach the height of perfection our spirit is created of.

Our spirit or feeling is our wisdom.

Our ego, sometimes referred to is soul, is our personality, our intellect, the student within us. It is the challenging, questioning curiosity of our wisdom.

Our feelings are deep within, eternal, immortal.

Our emotions are fluttering on the surface, they change from moment to moment depending on what is occurring on the outside. They are our human expressions.

Our bodies often pays the price for the disagreements between the first two.

1988. Visible signs of my life style
are written on my face.

Chapter 2

Learning to Live

I am sad. An innocent little statement. What does it mean?

Let's see:

Sad is an emotion. It is a reaction to something on the outside. Something my ego perceived as: 'I lost control somewhere along the way. It's not a real big deal, it's just a little one but I didn't get my way!' To be truly sad we droop our shoulders, hunch our backs, drop our heads, even frown our faces and mouths. We start to *sign* our emotions. We may even sigh, lower the tone of our voice, slow down the speed of our movements We stare into space, *space out*, etc., just to name a few physical displays that often accompany such emotion. We might even decide to go all the way and have a good cry! Of course we do not say: *"I permit myself to have the emotion of sadness and I am reflecting it through various signs throughout my body."* No way! People would think we are crazy! Instead, we say: "I'm sad." We *become our choice of emotion!* Naturally, we seldom stay in sad. Oh, no! We go way beyond that by becoming sadder while imagining a greater, more dramatic force of the original cause of *negative infusion* from the outside, intensify it, live it and farther depress our selves! Are we ever talented! All that, because the puppy has not yet grasped the idea of going onto the paper to do her natural potty business! We try to control the puppy's natural behavior by domesticating her - not a natural thing for an animal - and expect her to respond on our own time schedule, too! She doesn't know how to relate to our desire to control her body functions, because she does not yet have the *experience* of such *controlled behavior.* We lose control of both the puppy's actions and our own selves (feelings) and we develop an emotion called *sad*. Imagine how much fun we could have with the emotion *angry?* As we let go of our desire to constantly control ... emotions pass.

We have, for generations and generations inherited certain belief systems of our ancestors. Through evolutions of each generation we certainly made some minor and some major adjustments on these inheritances. There had been people who tried to rebuild some ancient natural beliefs only to be chastised and marked as weirdoes or idiots, insanes or geniuses. Some have been labeled as witches, even prophets, but for the majority, these labels had not been complementary. Most had indured rejection, public ridicule and physical pain. Some had been put to their death. Christ was one of them. Only a few were accepted for their courage to speak their new found truth. Sadly enough, most of those acknowledgments came long passed their lifetime, when they no longer had the opportunity to feel the joy of acceptance for expressing and delivering that truth. As for myself, I fall into two opposing categories of *angel* and *lunatic*, depending on the individual's perception of me at the time. Whenever I am cornered by rigid, closed minded people, I can only ask them: "How much trouble do you think Gallileo had, trying to sell his idea that our Earth is round, not flat? Things are not always what they seem to be. What I believe in is a piece o' cake!"

The reality is this: you can believe in whatever you want to and keep doing whatever you have been doing. If it works for you and you are content with the results then please, stick with it! On the other hand, if you have not yet reached that field where your spirit and your ego work and live together in harmony and for your highest good and well being, than it is my suggestion that you think about changing something. If you had tried and tried for years to arrive at a certain outcome and haven't as yet, chances are you are *thinking* and *doing* the very *same things* over and over again, receiving the very *same results*. It is insane to think that change will come from the same repetitious stagnation.

If we plant a pea seed into the ground we will harvest peas. If we keep planting pea seeds year after year, chances are we will become successful pea farmers. However, if we desire to harvest carrots, I'd suggest we plant some carrot seeds. Then, we nurture it, we tend to it, anticipate it. We wait patiently and lovingly, as we hand the details of growing over to God and trust in him. In its natural, perfect time, we will have our carrots in abundance!

Most of us had been taught to struggle for everything we desire. Yet, did we ever really do anything alone?

It is most important to have a desire, then decide what to do about it, make a total commitment to that decision, keep it in focus by putting your attention on it and just let go of it.

That is what I taught myself to do. My desire was to function better than I had been functioning in the past.
I decided to do all I could to become the best that I could be, by reversing the things that I previously did, which were: consuming unreasonable amounts of alcohol, smoking, eating irresponsibly, using mood altering drugs, (with or without prescriptions) and bouncing in and out of hurtful and abusive relationships. I committed my total self to this decision and I kept my focus on that commitment no matter who said what! I waited as patiently as I knew how, all the while repeating to myself that God and the universe were hard at work for me, figuring out the appropriate time and circumstances in which to reward me for my patience, belief and trust. It worked!

The first thing *I changed was the way I thought of me, myself.* I used to think that I was a miserable, used abused and worthless creature. Wrong!

"I am a one of a kind masterpiece of God's creation, filled with a lifetime of experiences and first hand information in dysfunction, perfectly and fully capable to recognize similar dysfunction in others and I am willing to guide anyone who is seeking to heal their own selves. I am grateful for my experiences."

This is a profoundly powerful, positive (if long) evaluation of who I am and how I think of myself now and how I believe myself to be, even though I still am the same person as I was before I made such a statement. Not only is it a true statement, it further clarifies my intention to extend myself to others.

In my time of full-blown egotistical arrogance, (even though I had no self - esteem) I thought and believed things like:

"I can do anything if I put my mind to it!" I would shout.

Today: "I surrender my body, my mind and my spirit to God. With God's love within me I accomplish my goals easily and effortlessly. I am grateful."

Before: "I know everything I need to know! Keep your opinions to yourself!" Aggressive, rude and disrespectful!

Today: "My wisdom is not my own. I speak wisely because God gives me his understanding. *All knowledge, information, everything comes from the same source. They come from God."* Humility is cost free and is never ending. I had to learn it and spread it around.

Before: "I don't have to listen to you! If I want to know something, I'll read a book, O.K.!"

Today: "I sit alone in the silence of my own making. I listen as God whispers his truth to me in-between my thoughts. *God's truth is universal. There can never be grater knowledge than God's.* Imagine a human creating an entire universe? I tried to and didn't get too far.

God is everywhere, in every thing, in every instant softly whispering to all of us through our spirits, whether we listen to him or not, admit him or not. The choice is ours to embrace him in our conscious mind or follow our ego and scatter about this planet aimlessly and without purpose until we perish like a thorn bird.

I am not writing about religion, rather I am writing about everything that is supposed to be in religion. All religions. I am writing about a power without which none of us could have life. I am writhing about God within you to call upon at any time, anywhere.

God. I am writing about God, the incredible, loving power of God, men's connection to God and the seed of God in each of us. Whether we like it or not, admit it or not.

We cannot see him, but he is there, everywhere. He is in the air, water, the sun rays, he is in you and in me. He was within me during my sorrowful and pathetic self-destruction, holding me up, waiting for me to call to him. He is with me now, deep within me day and night, when I am asleep and when I am awake, waiting for my desire, intention, decision, commitment and my attention.

Desire - Intention - Decision - Commitment - Attention.

The four most important ingredients in my own personal transformation.

What is *desire*? I used to think it was what I wanted. That was during my confused life.

A want is ego originated. A desire is in the spirit. Whatever we want we have to think about. It requires a great deal of effort. A desire is effortless and we do not need to consciously think about it nor can we consciously do anything about it. I desire to have my heart beat, so I can continue living life as I now am. The same goes for breathing. I cannot do much about it with my conscious mind, though. What will happen when I fall asleep? I would have to stay awake all the time! It is my spirit that keeps track of those important functions which my ego is incapable of. My spirit is always awake, even though it is silent, fulfilling my desire to keep living. Naturally, I must release this desire of staying alive, which I had done, usually at times when my ego realized that it went dangerously too far into the negative direction and was ready to panic, praying for life to go on, making false promises never ever to do this or that thing again! My spirit did hear my desire tough, and kept me alive. My intention was missing, so was my commitment. My attention scattered about, thinking and doing the same familiar things, arriving at the same old results.

So, have a desire and put your intention to it . It's wonderful to have a desire, but what are you going to do about it?

Make a *decision!* Decide on what your intention is. Are you going to do anything or are you going to ignore it. Release your desire. Let the universe and God know that you had made a decision on fulfilling your desire. If you keep holding onto it, keep it inside, that is exactly where it is going to stay: inside. Even though God is fully aware of your desire, it's nice to ask. You asked your parents, didn't you? They usually knew what you desired also, but most often they waited until you asked.

I'm not talking about begging or nagging God, either. Nor to keep reminding him of your desire. Just ask. Once is enough. Be clear, simple and precise. Let this desire come from your heart. Keep your focus on it and make this desire your intention. What ever you ask God to give to you, make it a single-mindedness of purpose beyond the shadow of any doubt. Believe in your purpose. Saturate your entire being with this desire. Finally, find yourself a quiet place and time, when you know that you will not be disturbed. Sit down and still your busy thinking mind. Still your mind. In-between your thoughts, in that space *Dr. Deepak Chopra* calls: gap, release your desire to God and the universe. I usually just take a deep breath and exhale as if I am blowing my desire out of my body and into the universe. (I was not consciously aware of this until someone once observed me in my meditation and later told me.) A certain feeling of lightness usually accompanies such a release. As I sit in my meditation, I always without fail, feel a sense of fulfillment and I believe with all of my being that God is smiling at me, taking joy in my own growth, knowing that I have evolved to be deserving of the fulfillment of my desire. I feel content and I know that everything needed for that fulfillment is already put into motion. I let go trustingly and gracefully.

I keep my full attention in focus and I never doubt or question that I am already being fulfilled.

I thank God for loving me and I am always grateful for everything I receive, from the air I breathe to the home I live in. I am grateful for the knowledge I receive from him and for sending me my clients who seek the fulfillment of their own desire and ask me to guide them along.

It is very important though, to be simple and precise about your desire and first be grateful for and be satisfied with what you already have. For instance, if you are desiring grater health, don't say:

"I am unhappy with my health." Chances are you will get sicker because God is eager to remove whatever is causing you unhappiness. Rather say:

"I am grateful for my health. It is my *dis - ease* and dysfunction, which I desire to let go of. *I am ready and willing to surrender all causes known and unknown to my conscious mind which are causing me the lack of total health. Thank you God for preparing me to receive total health and well being. I am grateful."*

Should your desire be more in the area of money (that commodity most of us seem to be in short supply of), don't ever say or even think that you are unhappy with your prosperity! I did and instead of receiving more, I lost the little I had in the first place!

Be grateful for what you have and ask to receive more.

There is nothing wrong with having all that you desire. God is our example of prosperity and abundance. Since God is creator of all that there is, all that there is belongs to God. If that is not prosperity and abundance than I don't know what is!

We are also created by God. Every one of us. He is our father, therefore we, each of us are his direct descendants. We are his children.

Believe it and accept it, because there is not a whole lot you can do to change it.

As our parent, it is God's desire is to fulfill all of ours. We need only to let him know that we are ready to receive.

At times I made the mistake in telling God when, where and how I would like to receive my goodies. I even gave him precise instructions. Soon I learned not to do that even if I meant to be helpful. As soon as I'd let go God knew it. I relaxed and learned to trust him. At the most appropriate time, when I least expected it, there it was. My gift from God. I am grateful.

Chapter 3

More Healing...

For most of my life I was led to believe that I was worthless, I was nothing. I was trained to settle for what I had because I didn't even deserve what I did have, so stop complaining, stop dreaming and wishing, sit down and be quiet! As a *good girl*, I did just that for a long, long time. Then, my little spirit, that all knowing part of me began her complaint, whispering different things to me like:

"You had been lied to! How much longer are you going to put up with all that garbage?"

Moment by moment my awakening strengthened.
I had to stop and listen if I were to stay alive. I left behind my old belief that I was nothing, deserved nothing. Today, I believe with all of my being that to live in sin is really to live in poverty, in lack, in sickness and in neediness rather than to live in peace and serenity, in prosperity and abundance.

My prosperity and abundance are the manifested expression of my closeness to God.

It is not my greediness at all! I am not speaking only of money either, though our ego part still holds on to the illusion that our wholeness and happiness are measured in monetary collectibles! I am now happier than I have ever been. Each morning as I awake, even before I open my eyes I affirm to God that we (God and I) are going to have the happiest, healthiest, most prosperous day ever! And we do! If you think I am kidding you, you are sadly mistaking this reality. I had been in the seven digit income bracket and in the .two digit, also. I had been able to manifest great things and prosperity in my life only to watch them sift between my fingers as I stood wondering what had happened. Why? Because I believed in my father's prophecy of:

"You will never amount to anything for as long as you live!" A belief which I had *inherited* from the man who projected his own personal lack into me from the very early stages of my life. Such statement had come from a person whom I believed in. As I began to *amount* to something, I soon found some way to sabotage my own success in order to fulfill his prophecy.

Through hypnotherapy Kathy found the key words to unlock my conscious, mental conditioning and reversed my understanding and perception of my life and people in it. With the continued use of the subliminal tapes, as I faithfully listened to them, I kept that understanding and positive belief mature inside of my mind until I was certain that the seeds of positive thinking were well rooted. I had reprogrammed myself to a happy, healthy and prosperous new me.

Could any of this transformation have taken place on its own accord? Could I have become a well person on my own at some future time? I don't know. Looking back and examining my own record, chances were pretty slim, from my new perspective. Deep in my heart I know the answer, which is a firm: no. All I am sure of in my conscious mind is that the way I healed was real. It worked for me.

Would it work for everyone else? Would it work for you, should you need healing? I can't answer that, either. It has worked, since I began my present practice in 1991, for 92% of my clients.

I am faced with much skepticism and criticism every day. It is good. Doubt is always good. Had I doubted my old reality sooner, perhaps my life would have been less dysfunctional. Perhaps not. That also does not matter today. What is most important is that if you had found a healing tool which you are certain is working for you than stay with it! If you haven't found it yet, than please keep

198

searching! Don't give up, because life is a bowl of cherries and you have every right to share in those cherries! Keep searching and you too, will find your very own Carla and Kathy. Do not, for another second believe that you must settle for pain, abuse, humiliation or poverty! You too, deserve the very best in life, because you too, are a child of God. A beloved, precious child born for an important purpose - to fulfill the continuum of life itself.

My dysfunction began with unnatural inputs from the outside and my full function began with natural awakenings deeply seeded in my inside. In reality they were always inside of me albeit locked up. The gentle reminders of the subliminal tapes gave me back my strength, my innate, natural, true realities. My ego finally surrendered to my spirit and said:

"I can't do this no more! (My ego also speaks with an accent.) I know I made a big mess of things over the years and now I don't know how to get out of it. I give up! Here, you fix it!" And she shoved the job over to my spirit to fix. So my spirit went to work and fixed it all she could. She's still working on it and has a permanent, full time job because my ego is in need of her constant guidance. The two of them get along very well now and my body radiates their cooperation. I'm glad.

As I got a firmer grip on what this human living is supposed to be all about, I started to feel different . More relaxed, more at ease, more at peace with life. Everyday events and people in my days did not affect me in the same way they used to. They simply did not affect me! I did not ignore them, quite the contrary! I became increasingly more aware of life around me. I started to see - perceive - everything differently. I no longer compared myself to anyone else nor did I measure my achievements (or lack of) to anyone else's achievements or expectations.

I accepted myself for precisely who I believed I was: virtues, wises, talents and lack of. *I started to live* from moment to moment, *in each moment*, enjoying life. I learned to love my moments and my life, realizing how very full they were. I gave up thinking about the negative things I used to do and how much of them I had done. Instead:

I concentrate on the positive things that I am doing right here and now in this moment.

Carla was constantly in my awareness. Kathy stayed with me for two months. I saw her twice or so a week for two months, through which time not once did she allow me to use her as my new crutch.

I finally understood that my feelings and emotions had very little to do with the world and people out there. They were the results of how I saw and perceived that world and how I chose to interpret that world. Everything had to do with my perception. Everything had to do with me! My well being had everything to do with me, the way I thought, not people or things out there somewhere!

Today I know, that what people think of me has nothing whatsoever to do with who I am. I am judged by their individual perceptions according to the labels which they tagged me with in the first place! We all are labeled by people, by culture, by society, by tradition.

Who I am is known only to God and me. I am a spiritual creation of God, living as his female image of me. My spirit is my god self. My soul is my human self. My strife is to bring those two parts of me into a vibration of harmonious union and live in Heaven on Earth - in this now tiny body of mine.

Discipline - another frightening word to dysfunctional humans - is also a major component in transformation. Once I learned to live in the present moment, I realized that I already had an abundance of discipline. As my ego surrendered its struggle for control, my discipline increased and I actually enjoyed it! The more discipline I exercised, the more of my spirit's beauty and talents shined through. Time was on my side for a change. The more I practiced the better I got and my transformation became visible.

It is important to note that not everyone around me was as thrilled with this transformation as I was. There were many people, still very much part of my daily life, who would have preferred to have me stay just as I was. The very same people, who themselves would have benefited by some of these changes I chose to make. They did not. It was not up to me to direct them one way or the other. It still isn't.

As part of growing out of dysfunction and into wellness, I had to allow myself to experience each and every newness.

I had to learn to consciously notice the changes and fearlessly surrender my entire being to the moment and God in every one of those moments.

A miracle slowly planted a tiny seed into the garden of my consciousness and blossomed into a beautiful, fragrant garden. I liked me! I began to cultivate this new garden and nurtured it into a precious thing of beauty, a new lifestyle. All I really did was desired to be the real me. What I received was a brand new true self of who I had been all through those years hidden behind a lot of drama.

I noticed feelings which I did not know I had.

Serenity. I no longer craved excitement.

Peace. The world out there was still the same: hectic, noisy, stressful, filled with demanding, rude, controlling people. My inside world was much more quiet than ever before.

Safety. I actually enjoyed being with myself! My negative temptations lessened and lessened as each day passed.   I missed nothing noticeable from my earlier lifestyle. I liked feeling the new way. My fears had melted.

When you live to your very best at each moment, you in fact, are the very best that you can be at that moment. That's a very safe feeling. You have nothing to worry about, nothing to fear because you are at your best. You can relax.

Moments pass by very quickly though, faster than a blink of an eye. This moment is already the past and I am already in the future that I'm sure of because I had not been here before! See how fast it is? Past, present and future are all in the present moment, entwined, interlocked and inseparable.

Our memories are from the past, our hopes and dreams are for the future but we all live in each instant of the present moment.

It had occurred to me that if I am being my very best in each and every moment (in my thoughts, my feelings, my words, my actions, etc.) than I am laying down a solid foundation to build both my past and my future on.

I let go of all the anxieties, guilt, shame and regrets of my past and had no fear of what the future would be - if there was such a thing is a future. I felt wonderful and I kept on practicing . No one else around me seemed to be overly exited about all this stuff, so I practiced alone. Today I don't have to do that anymore. Today I practice with hundreds of people around me.

Slowly, moment by moment my discipline grew and my ego became the student, not the teacher. My servant, not my master.

The light of my spirit began to flicker through. That little light started to shine on what used to be my big ego at places where it needed some polishing. It needed a lot of that! When I experienced uneasy emotions, I paid attention to the cause. Usually those were the areas where my ego needed some work. My ego no longer protested. It learned to trust and rely on my spirit. They formed a partnership and they're still working together, accomplishing much.

I paid close attention to people in my life, also. Not to judge them or compare them rather to observe them so I can learn more about them. I paid *attention* - something I hadn't done before. The more I watched them the more I understood myself. Since essentially we are all made of the same things and by the same God, we can easily mirror ourselves through others. We can recognize in others the qualities in ourselves which we do or do not like and correct them, if we choose to do so. We can discover areas for adjustments. Another opportunity for growth.

Some of the results of this new way of growing will take some time to become visible on the surface, but we are not too concerned with the surface, are we? We are more concerned with the inside of our selves.

Be patient. Another opportunity for adjustment.

When we live in the present moment, patience is always present.

My discipline grew and I had some temptations. *What is the value of discipline without temptation?* At each temptation I would take a small step backward and ask my ego if it was prepared to accept the responsibility for the outcome of the temptation. The answer invariably started with:

"I'm not sure," and ended in a definite: "No!"

We were creating peace, my spirit and my soul. My body functioned better as well. The old tremors left, so did the head-aches. The constant pain throughout my joints, which were forever present for as long as could remember, had lessened and in less than a year they too, had completely left. The adult acne which I had tried for years to clear up with various medicated creams, ointments and pills, also vanished and my complexion began to glow like never before. I had changed.

I spent a lot of time alone with my dog *Teddy,* as my only companion. Ted was great! He never complained about anything and loved me no matter what shape I was in, with and without makeup. I kept my contact with people limited to the hours that I spent at the gallery. I taught myself to be with me. No radio, newspaper or television, not even the telephone to distract myself from learning to be with me. It worked, although at first it was difficult, sometimes even terrible.

We are living in a society where we are constantly kept busy by one thing or another, having no awake time left to be with ourselves. We cannot learn very much about who we really are in the world filled with continuous distraction and entertainment.

What would we ever do, if we were faced with a week long national power shortage? No TV, radio, telephone, newspaper, no subway system, no lights after sunset, etc.! There would be chaos and panic and worse! We'd be forced to be in the dark, silent reality. We would have to be with our selves in the quiet darkness with our thoughts and emotions as companions. We would be forced to spend time in our own company! For some of us it is unimaginable but it can happen!

I learned to be with me without any outside entertainment. I learned to be quiet, even silent for long periods of time. I learned a new form of discipline. I practiced. None of this happened all at once.

First, I just sat quietly in a darkroom with my eyes closed for five minutes and couldn't shut my mind off. It did everything it could not to be quiet! Thoughts, images, memories form the past, ideas for tomorrow flashed through my mind, eager to distract my efforts of concentration to be blank and quiet. Those first five minutes seemed like five hours! I persisted. The following day I did the same routine for ten minutes! Same results. I persisted! By the time I reached a half hour of sitting alone and meditating, the first twenty minutes seemed to have quickly flown by! I persisted! Finally, I succeeded!

It is very important to mention here that my healing took time. It took me forty two years to become a successful dysfunctional person and only a little over a year to become well functional. To me the time was well worth it. I was scared and afraid at times, mostly in the beginning. I thought of abandoning the whole idea more than once, believe me. I looked for reasons and excuses to quit and return to the old and familiar ways of hurting myself. But I didn't. I realized, that there is no one but I, who can and must make these changes and I must change because I deserve to have a life filled with wonderful things, beyond my imagination. The noises, thoughts, images slowly left my mind and the anger, the fear, the guilt and doubt slowly left my emotions. I learned to sit quietly alone, being with only myself, without wanting to run away.

Today I am able to meditate in that same silence for many hours at a time irreguardless of what is going on around me.

*A moment of truth. Captured in frustration as
I tried to function as a designer. Early 1989.*

Chapter 4

Deeper Understanding

I had found beauty in things around me which I did not know had existed before...

Beauty is between sunrise and sunset and sunset and sunrise, both.
Beauty is for the ego to take a quiet bow in front of those creations over which it has no power - in contemplative silence.
Beauty is in the grace of humble acceptance.
L. Manonne Fontainne

As my new philosophy strengthened, my lifestyle shifted visibly. I couldn't boast of having lots of friends in the past and the ones I had found me *unusual.* Some of them labeled me *weird*. It was O.K. Day by day we drifted farther and farther apart. Even though I spent many years with some of them, without the alcohol in me I found very little in common with them. I didn't miss them. They did not share my enthusiasm about God nor did they care about my new theories on spirit and ego. I stopped going to places where alcohol was served, though I still kept some wine at my home. The metaphysical aspects of interpreting the Bible provided yet another focus and I was devoted to learn all that I could. I couldn't seem to get enough.

" Slow down," said Carla. "Don't create a new addiction for yourself!" I listened. She was right. I returned to more meditation but it didn't seem to be enough. I was experiencing withdrawal symptoms. My new life was new, unique and good and completely foreign to me. At times I questioned it. At times I didn't know what to do with it or in it! At times I was frightened of it, wondering how soon will all those good things slip away form me.

I liked not feeling bad - I did not understand feeling good!

I put my doubts aside and persisted. I undertook the project of ripping apart and remodeling my little 1903 home near the lake . I tore down walls and erected new ones elsewhere in the house. Out with the old and in with the new. The basic brown, orange and olive green little house slowly transformed into a spiritual haven of heavenly blues, lavenders, pinks and white. At the end, I was fully satisfied with the results - a home. My home.

Slowly and steadily I fell in trust and love with my new self, my new life and everything in it!

Each night I meditated any which way that I knew how. I relaxed and listened to the subliminal nature sounds on my cassette player. Teddy kept me faithful company. Teddy and I were making wonderful progress!

A year had passed - new people entered my life - people who shared my beliefs. We tested each other and accepted each other. Carla was genuinely happy for me. Kathy suggested that I consider and study hypnotherapy.
I thought about her suggestion and pictured myself being one, working with people, guiding people. It felt good.
I enrolled. One evening I thought I heard God say:
"You must learn more about me." How could I have refused God? I studied about God.

By early fall in 1990 Kathy let me practice on some of her willing clients. I found my life filled with life and I was passionate about it. Beauty and joy were everywhere

208

around me and within me. I learned to accept and allow myself to feel good. I no longer waited for something to go wrong. I felt the meaning of the word: joy!

Carla said to me:

"Sugar, you are on your path." I agreed with her. On a late September afternoon in 1990, as I was taking a solitary walk on the sandy beach of Lake Coeur d' Alene, I glanced back and saw that my footprints were still there, following me behind.

"I have a ways to go," I said out loud with the smile of a child.

I was still drinking on occasions.

Emotions surfaced on the daily basis but they no longer intimidated me. I kept repeating the familiar affirmation:

"...all emotions pass....all emotions pass....'

Each time I felt some un-ease creep upon me I took a tiny step backward. That small and seemingly meaningless act allowed me to remove myself from the very space where I was sensing the imbalance. That action also gave me just enough time to figure out what was causing this un-ease before I acted or reacted in defense or impulse. Not surprising, I found that the internal commotion once again had been caused by my ego, finding a chance to compete or looking for some argument. I assured and mellowed out the little trouble maker and relaxed. My method worked. The emotion passed without any disturbance or discomfort.

No more problems, only opportunities in which to learn and grow.

There were challenges to overcome and new lessons to learn. Pieces of puzzles to arrange and put into their correct places.

"Sure," you'd say, but it is true. I have no problems in my life. Within only a year, all areas of my life had converted itself into something new, something I previously had no idea that I could experience with ease or better yet, like living! My friendships and associations with people changed. I surrounded myself with those who understood and shared my healthier beliefs. I was content. I still spent a lot of time alone with my little white dog as my sounding board. Teddy patiently listened to anything I had to say and accepted my new self. He showered me with his genuine love through meaningful, if very wet doggy kisses. At nights he'd jump up on my bed and curl up into a little white ball at the foot of it. We slept in peace.

No more nightmares or lurking midnight monsters to disturb our rest.

I still drank some wine. Some, not very much.
I introduced my word game to my new friends and we had lots of fun. We grew together, played together.

Hope, hopelessness - not feelings but states of mind.

Perception - the way my ego sees, judges and interprets the world outside of myself Very good!

Anger, hate, jealousy - emotions caused by my ego while struggling for control. Poor thing, that ego!
I continued on track.

Honesty - surrendering to truth. That was a hard one. Addicts are gifted, master liars, deceivers and manipulators and they can keep busy day and night, covering up their tracks. I know, I used to be one of them!

Surrender - the letting go of old beliefs, old habits, old memories, old emotions. Letting go of the past and allowing the unknown, the untried, the un-experienced reality to flow into your whole being. Letting go of the slow death of daily self destruction and expectations.

Letting go and surrender are two of the tunnels toward the light of total transformation.

With each discovery into my inner self I rewarded myself with a live plant. Soon I was in need of a larger home! There were times when I wondered: 'How did I ever survive before?' It didn't matter anymore! I was living in the present moment. I still needed some discipline:

Don't look back, look forward. Concentrate on the things you are now doing - rather that what you did!'

I kept playing with my words, writing them down over and over again.

Desire - purity of spirit.

Intention - what to do about my desire.

Decision - selecting a choice with clarity of mind.

Commitment - an irreversible state of discipline.

Attention - a constant awareness.
I added some new ones:

Attitude - a state of mind.

Purpose - taking an active part in living life, itself.

Serenity - a feeling of completeness.

GOD - purest form of creative energy, creator of all that is manifest and un-manifest throughout our entire universe. The power of pure love and immeasurable potential beyond human comprehension. Creation.

GOD---Go On Doing.

A new friend presented me with a tiny medallion of a Yin Yang. Two fishlike symbols, one black and one white, shaped into a circle. He said it was a Chinese interpretation of our feminine and masculine aspects. I was grateful for the gift. As I kept looking at it, the medallion had a completely different meaning to me. I recognized in it *our light and dark sides. Spirit and soul. Good and evil.* How wonderful it was to see my theory of spirit and soul brought into a perfect balance and encircled within its own self! I realized that I had to surrender my new *discovery* to something called*: ancient wisdom.* Oh, well.

Balancing our spirit and our soul is the only answer to healing and rising toward divine consciousness.

A year or so before these ideas, even if they were someone else's, would have intimidated me. By then I was at the level of my healing where I could relax with pretty much all of my thoughts, even the unusual ones. They frequently flashed across my conscious awareness and often seated themselves there for a time . Many of them I really did not understand, yet. It was O.K. I figured that they were hidden little clues from God to be used at some later time.

I wondered and pondered about religion and spirituality . My awareness was being cultivated without any effort. One morning I awoke with a new perception of me:

I am a one of a kind masterpiece created by God as his female expression of perfection of me, not to be compared with any other masterpiece of his creation. A child of God, a descendent of an immortal entity - God. A direct heir in his Kingdom of Heaven on Earth. A web woven from the threads of pure love, peace, joy, serenity, freedom and much more, into eternal spiritual life. That is who I am. That is who you are!

My *awareness* took on a new light of its own. Pure awareness is a relaxed state of being, when our attention is limitless, free and non judgmental. It is perception without decision based on any particular belief. It is awareness without attachment. Pure awareness also requires a little practice of acceptance.

Acceptance is the key to the front door of a new lifestyle. As my ego relaxed and allowed more of God's presence into my moments, my acceptance grew and I truly relaxed in my life . The very first thing I needed to accept was me. Believe it or not, that was the most difficult thing to do! One evening as I was practicing my meditation, a thought came to me:

'Forgive.' Carla had often told me to forgive and so did Kathy. I had no idea of what or who to forgive or how to do that at the time. There was something different about this thought, though. This one was more like a message coming from somewhere at the back of my mind. A soft, whispering voice filled with compassion:

"Forgiveness is not for those whom you believe had wronged you. Forgiveness is for you to free yourself of those emotions which you hold as grudges against the wrong doers. Forgive and you will be free to feel joy and peace and freedom yet unknown to you. Punish yourself

not a moment longer with your emotions of anger and hate and revenge. Everything is as should be."

I've heard that before! My eyelids flew open, expecting to find someone sitting in front of me . I was alone with only my dog Teddy laying by my side. He was peacefully asleep. That night I had a dream . A very unusual dream. In this dream I was standing someplace near Heaven. There were many, many others, also standing and waiting around quietly, all of them dressed in long, white toga - like garments that reached all the way down to their feet. I was wearing one of my pink sweat suits and stood a little to one side, not really being part of the crowd. As I looked ahead I saw a white gate, much like the movable arm at a toll booth and in front of the gate there was a figure standing, also dressed in white who looked like he might have been in charge. He was. He was St. Peter and the gate was the gate to Heaven. I noticed that a small figure appeared in front of St. Peter. He bent down and whispered something to the small figure. Slowly, the figure turned around and looked directly at me and I saw that it was my grandmother! I waved to her excitedly and she waved back to me. Then, with a smile ever so loving she turned away. The gate opened and she walked through it. I had the most beautiful, most peaceful feeling, a feeling which lingers around me even today. The gate lowered again. Before I had a chance to think about her, I saw three new figures standing in place of my grandmother. St. Peter bent down once again and whispered something to the three of them. All three lowered their heads and suddenly three angels appeared and stood behind them. As they turned sideways, I recognized each of them: my father, my uncle and the father of my son. The gate never opened and they did not get to go through Heaven's gate. The angels led all three of them away to the right and out of my sight.

214

When I awoke the following morning, the dream seamed to me more real than life itself. I clearly understood and accepted the meaning of forgiveness. It was not up to me to pass judgment over someone else's right or wrong doings. There was something somewhere far beyond me and my abilities to decide on such important matters. Forgiving them came as natural to me as did breathing. As I forgave them, I was able to let go of many of my emotions, making room for my beautiful feelings. Much of my burden lifted that morning and I felt, for the first time, truly free. I understood then *that freedom is not a place but a state of being.*

Today, I know that forgiveness does not mean excusing or denying the reality of other people's hurtful doings. It means letting go of our emotions about their actions. We, all of us have the right to choose to be with or without those who are harmful to us on any level. Perhaps not as little babies, but as we grow older and more into our conscious awareness, we all have the power within our selves to select choices for our safety and continual happiness.

Since then I live my life without judgment, while being fully aware of everything in every moment in this life which I manifested. Harsh, seemingly rude, angry people teach me to be kind, gentle and even *more accepting but not settling.* It is easy to walk away with love and prayer in my heart and a pure desire for them to find the wisdom of God. Each and every person who I come in contact with plays an important part in my life which I may or may not recognize and understand in the moment of encounter - more important than my imagination can ever provide me with.

With the key of acceptance in hand I walked through the door that led me into my new, healthy life and there I live, *one moment at a time.*

Meditation and prayer.

Chapter 5

Choices

Following both the advice of Kathy and my own desire, I continued with my hypnotherapy studies. I liked all the things I was learning and everything fit wonderfully well into my new beliefs. My own personal healing - for which I give hypnotherapy and subliminal therapy a great deal of credit - had been a deciding factor in selecting this profession for myself.

Before I had a chance to finish my studies, I enrolled in ministry school. After careful selection, my choice became: The International Assembly of Spiritual Healers, a non-denominational congregation of spiritual healers around the world. I finally found the place where I belonged: in the constant presence of God.

To me, being a minister means to be in a full-time service of God and you. My ministry is not a title or flag to wave at you but a gentle reminder for me - of the direction I chose to walk in. My ministry is not for other people. *My service is.* Each time I scribble those three little letters in front of my name: rev., I remind myself of the path I found and choose to follow, the commitment I silently made to nurture you and to look with you for your own key to unlock the door to your own spirit, your own inner wisdom - should you ask me to. I wouldn't want to do anything else.

We've come a long way: my spirit, my ego and my body . People came and went, emotions came and passed, dis - eases came and eased. I lived my life in a state of tranquillity while being fully aware of the world around myself - near and far. I learned to meditate to hear my inner self, rather that to escape from the outer world. I learned to accept and love myself and I learned to freely and willingly give love to all without ever asking:

"So, what's in it for me?"

I learned that I was O.K. exactly the way I was no matter what other people thought of me.

When an old friend asked:

"Don't you care about what other people think of you?" An answer from thin air gushed out:

"Do any of those other people ever wonder what I may think of them?" I was no longer enslaved to judgment, worry or fear. Other people had plenty stuff of their own to be concerned about. I learned to hear, listen, offer and receive without taking someone else's burden's away from them and making it my own. I learned to help and guide, not fix. I learned to *help* only when I was asked.

A voice moved in with Teddy and me. A voice without the body and it kept talking to me during most of my meditations. I kept hearing that it was time to pack, I was going to move. I didn't want to move! I just started to find some sanity and stability and now I was moving? Where to?

"You are going East," said the voice in my head.

"East? Everyone else is moving West and I am going East? No way!" I answered myself.

"You are going East," spoke the voice peacefully.

I ignored the message and continued to work at the gallery, on my home and kept to my studies. By this time, my little home looked as though a bomb hit it! A simple job of remodel turned into a major reconstruction and I was doing all the labor. I started to feel eight feet under. The truth is, I still needed to create some stress and chaos in my environment, even though I was not yet consciously aware of such a need at the time. I was still manufacturing plenty of adrenaline and needed to keep busy to wear it off. Since all other areas of my life progressed smoothly, I seemingly needed the confusion to keep the memory of the experience active. I hadn't quite learned to accept total tranquillity. It too, came in its right time.

Adam and I parted amicably. Once in a while, he still called and asked me to join him for dinner. I declined. He asked me to go on a vacation with him to Hawaii. I declined. In the twelve years we spent together I learned and remembered enough to know that we would soon return to playing the games with each other which we both learned to do so well. I knew that I didn't want to play - I didn't know how to do anything else yet in a relationship. I stayed away.

We divorced and I received my gallery, my little home and the T'bird. Adam received the rest of the seven figures of wealth we manifested. It was O.K.

Weeks, months passed by and I found more and more peace within myself. I kept to the safety of my business and my home. Friends came to visit me. I was content, even happy at times. It didn't occur to me that I was isolating myself from the world and my security was limited to my immediate environment. I escaped the reality of the world outside into the safety I created for myself. I was still learning.

A year and a half after my moment of awakening (in May, 1989) I was feeling good, I was on my own, free of drugs (both legal and illegal) and I no longer got drunk. Once in a while I drank some wine, mostly when I was with *other people*, but I did not need to get drunk anymore. Once or twice I was asked out on a date by both old and new acquaintances. I declined until one evening as I was working late at my office, a close friend knocked on my window motioning for me to let him in. I did. My office was located at the back of the gallery and as I led him to it, he held onto my arm and stopped me in the middle of the store.

"I need to say something to you before we go any further." Said Sven. I stopped to listen and there in the semi darkness, shortly after my divorce, I received the most sensitive love confessions of my life. After he was done, we both just stood there motionless. I didn't know what to do with him and his words. I was numb in my confusion and surprise, hearing such endearing words from a man I could only perceive as a friend. I told him so as gently as I knew how.

"You'll change your mind, I know you will." It was October, 1991.

Sven was the first person who knew me before and after, and came forward to say how proud he was of me for having the strength to stand on my own. I fell for it. Each morning he brought me a steaming hot cup of coffee and when my assistant came in to work, we went for a casual morning walk. He was right, I was changing my mind.

After work I went home to my dog and meditation. During the day I listened to Sven, at nights I listened to the voice without the body:

"You are going East." The voice would whisper.

"No, I'm not." I would answer.

"You are wonderful." Sven would compliment.

I heard about my virtues, my values, my sweetness, my strength. And yes, I still heard about my beauty, too.

I yielded and we developed a short but intense relationship of impossibility. If I didn't have enough chaos and stress in my life earlier, I certainly got plenty again. Having known dysfunction and instability all of my life I recognized it just as soon as I was in it. I still didn't know how to prevent it or how to get out of it! I was still learning.

Sven and I created a business together only to loose it all at the end. He came to my home to help me with the remodel and he meditated with me. I heard the voice without the body say:

"You are going East." When I mentioned it to Sven he panicked and we argued. The voice was persistent and we argued more and more. I was no longer at peace or happy. Business suffered and I lost most of the money that I made earlier. In many areas Sven was wonderful: he was sweet and kind. He was very supportive of me in my transformation and often studied with me, primarily the spiritual parts. His own insecurity caused him to be possessive and I was not offering myself to be his crutch. I was not completely healed yet and I didn't know how to began healing him.

Among all of my newly created mess, I found something outstandingly different:

My situation did not effect me as it would have a few years earlier. It was O.K. I truly believed that whatever I was experiencing had an important purpose which I had yet to understand and would in the future. I didn't panic, I was not fearful and I did not try to control or change Sven. I accepted everything in my situation but I did not allow myself to become a victim nor did I settle for that situation!

We parted. I was not in pain and I did not wonder if I could have done this or that differently and how else could have things evolve if I did do this or that, this way or that way. What was, was and it was completed. I was still learning.

The pieces of the puzzle of my life slowly fell into place. My ordination came first. As I took a step as a *minister* I became a *spiritual healer* as well. Soon after, I received my *hypnotherapy certification* from the National Guild of Hypnotists.

As stress left, peace and tranquillity returned.
I was sure it would!

*Lecturing at the luncheon of the C. R. Chapter of
The American Cancer Society.*

Chapter 6

More Learning...

Early in 1992 I sent away for an album of cassette tapes by *Anthony Robbins* titled: *Unlimited Power*, through Nightingale Conant. A couple of weeks later I received a package. I opened it with excitement only to find a wrong set of tapes in the box! I was disappointed, got on the phone, called Nightingale Conant and told them so! I wanted them to send me the tapes I ordered. The woman at the other end of the line listened patiently, apologized for the mix up, assured me to correct the mistake and suggested that I keep the ones I received and if I choose, I am free to listen to them while the others were on their way. I felt satisfied with her calm response and took her advise. I turned on my stereo, opened the box and went speechless. The album was placed upside down in the box and there was a photo of a handsome Indian man with the warmest, deepest dark eyes looking straight up at me, as if he was there in person. I pulled back but I couldn't take my eyes off of the photograph. I just set there on my living room carpet in front of my stereo looking at that photograph.

'Who are you?' I wondered. I hadn't watch TV for a long time and I really had no idea who that person could be. Tears filled my eyes and I had one of those feelings which I felt many more of as time passed by. A confusing, but good, fuzzy feeling. When I composed myself I read the title of the album:

Magical Mind, Magical Body by Deepak Chopra, MD

I automatically held the album to my chest and for no apparent reason said: "Thank you."

I played all six tapes, all twelve side without ever getting up. I understood every thought, every idea, every word that was recorded onto those narrow little brown tapes. Thoughts, ideas, truths that Carla and Kathy, even my transitioned grandmother had been teaching me, but couldn't put into such an eloquent presentation as did Dr. Chopra.

I sat quietly and peacefully for a while, knowing that everything from then on was going to be wonderful no matter what awaited me. When it was time to sleep, I took the tapes and tucked the whole album under my pillow. Once, I jokingly said to my daughter:

"I slept with the greatest doctor in the world!"

(Under no circumstances should this sentence be miss-understood, miss-used or miss-quoted by anyone, at any time for any purpose!)

The next morning, as soon as my work allowed it, I went on a hunt and shopping expedition to buy everything that was available written and recorded by Dr. Deepak Chopra. I was calm and full of purpose. I read and understood his writings. I flew around the country to attend his lectures each time he promoted a new book.

When he finally came to Spokane, Washington, several of my friends came with me to hear him. In fact, a friend even bought the ticket for me. After the lecture, the crowd stood around in a long line to have him autograph their books and I dared to be one of the groupies. As my turn came, I said to him:

"I didn't bring a book with me. Can I give you a hug, instead?"

"Of course," said Dr. Chopra. He put his pen on one of the steps of the stage where he was sitting at, stood up, placed his palms together, graciously bowed then looked at me and gave me a gentle hug He radiated the most wonderful, calming energy one simply cannot write about, only feel. When we let go, he carefully lifted the bangs on my forehead and smiled. (I wore and still wear a golden star on my forehead which was placed there as I was ordained to be a minister, as a reminder to always go forward and follow God's golden light, also to help me learn to overcome the constant judgment and criticism of humanity, at all cost.)

On my the way out of the lecture hall I wrote my name and address on the mailing list thinking nothing of it, really. We had a wonderful evening after the lecture. Many of my friends came over to my home and we talked for hours, exchanging our thoughts, feelings and excitements about Dr. Chopra's presentation of his newly released book: *Ageless Body, Timeless Mind.*
We all had a copy and made use of it.

I returned to my real life of work, study, meditation and listening to the voice without the body. A few weeks passed and I received something from Sharp Institute in *San Diego, California*, probably as a result of my registering on the mailing list. At first I thought:

'More junk mail, another tree cut down. Why did you even leave your name!' I read the mail, though. Well, there was nothing junky about that mail! It was an invitation to study with the great doctor!

I was on my way! I drove to San Diego, California (the same city I once called my home) to hear and learn all that *Dr. Deepak Chopra and Dr. David Simon* were willing to share. They shared and I soaked it up like a thirsty sponge. I learned from other doctors as well:
Dr. Richard Snyder and Dr. Jeremy Geffen, Dr. Vasant Lad and Dr. Candace Pert, among a few.   I learned about alternative and complimentary healing of body and mind through the immeasurable power of spirit.

I learned about the doshas and how to identify each; Ayurvedic concepts from consciousness to matter;

nutrition; yoga; the yoga of herbs; aromatherapy; purification procedures; the function of the quantum mechanical framework for healing; psycho-neuro-immunology in mind/body healing; restful alertness; about the powerful role of the mind in the construction and destruction of body cells and the entire human body.

Body - Mind - Spirit.

The lecture room was filled with wonderful healing energy just from the presence of the people. I have yet to see Dr. Chopra on any of the many television shows he appears on. I can tell you though, that to experience the great doctor's presence in person day after day, from morning to evening is quite something else. He never seemed to tire and sharing his limitless knowledge with all of us seemed to be most important to him at the time. He is a quiet, soft spoken man filled with unique knowledge, courage and wisdom yet to be found elsewhere in our time. That education was the best investment of my life.

I also found myself in the company of some of the greatest medical and scientific minds of our time. My next seat neighbor was our beloved *Dr. Benjamin Spock.* (Dr. Spock assigned me the job of kicking him, should he fall asleep. When I failed to do so, he kicked me!) I considered myself most fortunate, as I remembered the place, space and level of consciousness I was at only a couple of years before.

On the last day of my study, Dr. Chopra came up to me, lifted my bangs off my forehead and smiled:

"I thought it was you," he said and someone took a picture of us. I was honored that he recognized me from our brief meeting in Spokane, Washington.

"Doctor Chopra, I need your guidance. Where do

I go from here and now?" Our lectures were over and I felt a sense of loss, a lack of direction.

"Manonne, God gave you a special kind of voice. Use it."

That's all he said to me. He smiled, turned and walked away, leaving me to figure out what he ment. In time I did. Today, I am doing just that and I am going to keep on doing it for the rest of my natural life.

On my way home as I was driving through Southern Idaho, I got stuck in a winter blizzard. Visibility was poor, the road icy and winding high up in the mountains, near the town of McCall. At a curve in the road I noticed a deer or elk walking in front of me, so I tuned the wheels of the car to avoid hitting the animal. I guess, I turned it too far, because it ran up the cement road guard and I totaled my beloved T'bird, making the front end look like an accordion Other travelers behind me thought I was dead and gone but I walked away without a scratch although shook up. The local hospital would not even consider keeping me for an overnight observation. A nurse, who was going off duty drove me to the nearest town and I stayed at a hotel.

As I was dozing off, the voice without the body spoke:

"Everything is as it should be. You are going East."

'You have got to be kidding me! Right now nothing is well and I am not going anywhere! I don't have a car anymore, remember?' I answered my mind. 'First, I gotta get home.'

"Soon, you are going East, soon."

Soon 'is fine. Now I'm going to sleep!'

Another lecture. Cedar Rapids Public Library.

Chapter 7

Miracles...

Early on the afternoon of June 16, 1993 I had an appointment to see my local doctors about a lump in my right breast which, once again I manifested. We've been watching it since September of the year before and lately it had changed its size and shape, so I took it more seriously. I was on my way, driving to the appointment when a car pulled onto the road from a side parking lot and hit me head on! Another accident! It happened so fast there was nothing I could do to avoid it. I hit my head and suffered a tiny cut on my inner lip. Seeing the blood someone called for an ambulance. They pried me out of the car and off I went to the hospital, missing my other appointment. I went through the normal emergency procedure of questions, pokings and X-rays. There was nothing broken but this time I was in a lot of pain. I was sent home with lots of pills, a traction and instructions:

" Stay in bed, don't do this, that and the other thing, take your medication, call your attorney and insurance agent..." With the help of friends I did and didn't do them all. I had lots of time to reflect on my life: past and present and for the first time I allowed myself to remember my childhood, my growing years and the people and things I had left behind. I discovered that I was no longer afraid nor ashamed of my past. Whoever I was, was the result of my past experiences.

During my *chemical era* a friend said:

"It's her karma..." I think what he ment to say was that I was supposed to be and stay a *victim of my selfabuse.* I believe it different. My karma was not to be a chemical goddess, but to recognize, overcome and correct my addictions, then teach others to do the same should they choose to heal themselves. The lesson I had to learn was not how to be the best drunk but how to crawl out of the bottle, stand straight, grow strong and gracefully walk away, never looking back. I thought of the story of the phoenix... flying away, never looking back.

Not looking back does not mean to deny what was. It means not missing it, not yearning for it, not dwelling on it.

"Don't look back. Walk forward with a new bounce in yours stride, a new yearning in your heart, a new commitment in your mind and a new song on your lips. Addicts and co-dependents are wonderfully committed, durable people. They have staying power and they will go to any length, at any cost to fulfill their commitment! Use that same staying power in your commitment to be clean, to be free of all your self - destruction.

As I lay there not understanding but accepting my latest miss-hap, I knew that I could have indulged myself in serious pity. I was in pain, I couldn't work, I was losing money, etc. I had long before liquidated my art and antique business to pay bills. I had a small hypnotherapy office which I opened in my home and I gave my best to treat everyone with the best of my conscious awareness and professional training. I was earning a modest but satisfying self support from it.

Financially, there was much to be concerned about but I knew that worrying would make things worse not better. I learned to relax with my pain and gave my body every opportunity to get well. As I lay in bed, my thoughts drifted toward the desire to let go of the lump. I didn't want any more attention because of some drama in my life. I yearned for attention through my new health and clarity of mind. I focused on my wellness.

Within a few weeks I was up and around, able to pick up where I left off. When I returned to the doctor to check on the lump, he couldn't find it!

"Doctor 'H', can I tell you what I think had happened?" I asked him. He picked up one of the crystals I wore around my neck, rolled it between his fingers and said:

"No. I am a man of science, Manonne. I'm not suppose to know about things like that." He let the little rock gently fall back onto its resting place on my chest and gave me a hug. I had tears in my eyes. He did in his.

I don't know if the lump I had was malignant or benign. We didn't get as far as testing it. I do know, that it left my body, hopefully forever and it was good enough for me.

I returned to meditation and very soon I manifested a few clients. Then, more and more clients came and soon I was busy doing what I now know is my life's purpose.
I noticed that most of the people I worked with were primarily chemical dependents and co-dependents, though I hypnotized quite a lot of clients suffering from depression and stress, even mid-life crisis and low self-esteem. Though many of them never paid me for my services, my rewards came from the wealth of experiences I gained which I now apply to my clients' benefits today.

At that present time, I specialize in these areas and cannot imagine myself doing anything else. It is quite an experience to see a person stagger into my office loaded up on something, having drank or used for many decades than watch him or her walk out of the same office only a few months later as a new, stable, independent self.

Not everyone made it. There had been a few number of clients who returned to their old commitments. Some of them came to listen at my spiritual services and a few of those finally made their transformation into a clean life. Some did not.

In my free time I meditated and yes, you guessed, listened to the voice without the body:

"You are going East."
'All right, already, I'm going, I'm going! When?'
'Soon. You are going East, soon."

Early morning, on August 16, 1993 neither John nor I had any idea how different our lives will become before the day was over. John didn't know that he will be taking his brother's place on a trip to Coeur d' Alene, Idaho and I didn't know that I will finally discover the destination of the: "You are going East" message.

It had been a long, long time, since I entered a bar, but on that fateful day I was meeting a girlfriend in the cocktail lounge of a popular, downtown restaurant. What was most amazing is that it was *my* idea to meet there and I was insistent. My friend and I met and had a nice time visiting for a while, then she became deeply involved in a conversation with a person seated next to her. I started to get a little antsy and thought of going home, so I softly poked my friend, Velma at her side to get her attention She pulled away and continued to ignore me, so poked her again. Still, she ignored me. Finally I leaned across the bar and at that very same moment another person did the same and I found myself looking into the purest blue pair of eyes God ever could have created. I sat back on my chair and I new that there was something significant going on, something I didn't understand . When I leaned forward again, those blue eyes were still there.

Can you remember back to the time when you met someone, whom you were sure was going to be significant in your life? You broke out in a sweat, felt light headed with a thousand butterflies dancing in the pit of your stomach and you couldn't find your own voice, never mind say something intelligent! Nothing like that happened to me. Instead, I felt calm. More calm than ever before, as if I just came home to safety from a lifetime of battle. My feelings were as peaceful and unruffled as the ocean's surface when all breeze had subsided. The only disturbance was the echo in my own mind:

"You are going East."

'Will you be quiet, already! Not now!' I silently chided myself.

"Manonne, this is John, John, this is Manonne. John is here on business from Iowa." My friend Velma introduced the owner of the blue eyes.

"Hello, John. Where exactly is Iowa from here?" I asked.

"Its East of here," said John.

"You are going East," said the voice without the body.

'Oh, no! Not so soon!' I thought.

"Yes. You are going East."

"I am going to marry you." I heard my own voice say and then I felt my whole body turn beet red from the top of my head to the tip of my toes, as I blushed.

"Hello, Manonne. I believe you are right." John answered.

The following month I met John's parents and other members of his family. I couldn't tell if they liked me or not. I couldn't care less. I was going East.

I completed my home and decided to sell it. I worked with my clients, often wondering what will happen to them after I leave. I found a way to teach them independence. I was at peace. John called me daily and several times a day. He wanted to know about my life, my beliefs, my faith, the God, whom I deeply loved by then. We talked about which one of us should be relocating At nights, the voice kept repeating:

"You are going...."

'You can relax now. I know, I am going East.' I interrupted the voices of my mind. I was ready to go East. I was at peace.

The night of October 3, 1993 was a personal history maker, tough what you will read is not from my memory.

I will write the event as it was related to me by my friend, Catherine. Earlier that evening John and I agreed that
I will drive to Iowa the following morning, which I did after a chain of strange events. I invited Catherine to stay at my home while I was gone, to watch over Teddy and my jungle of tropical plants. She was glad to do it. I had gone to bed early in the evening so I would be fully rested for the 1600 or so mile drive going East to Cedar Rapids, Iowa. I fell to sleep almost immediately and the rest is Catherine's story:

"Around 9:00 PM you got out of bed and kept walking about your house as if you hadn't been there before. You kept walking into the furniture, mostly your dinning table over and over again, as if it wasn't there or if you were suppose to be able to just walk through them. You couldn't of course and it puzzled, even annoyed you. I was laying on the sofa and once you kind of wobbled over and said something which I couldn't understand. At first I thought you were talking in one of your foreign languages but you weren't really talking, more like guttering. I told you that I didn't understand you. Then you came over to me, bent down only inches from my face and asked who I was. I said my name and all you said was: *'Oh.'* Then you turned and walked away, opened the door to the china cabinet and took out a few things, but instead of putting them back, you just dropped them on the floor. You got a bunch of broken things, kid! At that point Kelly (my daughter also stayed in my house for the night) packed up the baby and took off around 9:30 PM. She said you were back in the bottle again and she was really mad at you as she left. Around 10:00 PM or so, I was able to get you back to bed and you agreed to eat something. I heated up some chicken soup and when I put it in front of you, you didn't seem to know what to do with it. You kept looking at the spoon, then finally said: *'you eat funny'*. I got you to lay down in bed, only to find you waking around again, this time without any clothes on. I called Velma. She drove over and together we managed to put you back into bed once again . She was going to call for an ambulance but

I figured, if Kelly was right and you were drunk, you'd probably end up in trouble and it isn't going to look very good and you're gonna need to sober up anyway, so I didn't let her. You kept asking us where you were at and we kept telling you: at home. I don't mind telling you, all that was a little weird and I was confused. Around 2:00 AM you finally stayed in bed and settled down. Velma left and I got a little sleep. Do you do this sort of thing often?" Catherine was telling me these things the following morning as I hurried, getting ready to leave. I stopped, looked at her and said:

"Catherine, I don't remember a thing of what you just told me. I can't believe I broke all these things! I collect swans and doves, why would I want to destroy them?" I had no memory of that night. Not then, nor ever since. I couldn't tell if she just fabricated some off the wall story for our amusement or she was telling me the truth. I didn't think any more about it. I do know that many unusual events occurred to me since that night.

I was late to leave and found myself rushing.
I already knew that the trip will have to be made in one continuos drive to be there by Wednesday at 5:00 PM. It was Tuesday at 10:00 AM. I had to drive 1600 plus miles.

I am not a good driver, nor a bad one. I'm just a driver with a particular destination and usually some deadline to meet, always pressed for time. There was a lot on my mind to keep it form thinking about my escapade of the night before. I was going East. Finally! I was meeting John on his turf. I was hoping to find some other reason to go East. Some hidden message from the voice without the body.

In the middle of Wyoming as I looked down to the digital readout of my car (another T'bird), it showed 0 gallon to empty!

"Oh, no! This can't be happening to me! I'll never make it on time now!" I fell disappointed, near tears. There was nothing around me to indicate human life. No towns, no farms, no homes, not even an abandoned barn. I could see for miles into the green, rolling hills and not find a moving thing. There wasn't even a breeze that day! I felt deflated. All I could do was pray to God to please, put whatever little sub-atomic particles gas is made of into my gas tank so I could get to the nearest gas station, some-where!

I don't know what is considered a miracle but what I experienced after that, in my point of view could very well qualify as one. I looked back to the very same digital panel of the car and instead of 0, it indicated: 1 gallon left to empty. Than 2, 3, 4, 5, 6, 7 gallons to empty. It didn't go higher than 7. I drove for quite a while, amazed! When I looked ahead I saw smoke drifting toward the sky in the distance. I knew that there had to be some fuel there or near there. I headed in that direction, taking a big chance at leaving the freeway and turning onto a dirt road. The digital numbers began to drop one by one and fast, once again showing 0, as I reached the source of the smoke. Sure enough, there was a farm home with the only gas station for another 80 miles - the young man informed me, as he filled the tummy of my T'bird with 27 gallons of fuel!

"Golly, Lady, yo' shur' got a big tank under that fancy car o' yo'rs! Where yo' goin' anyways?" The young man was passing time, making conversation.

"East. I am going East," I said to the young man, and I watched him pump 27 gallons of fuel into a 20 gallon gas tank and paid him for the 27 gallons. Miracle or my imagination? I didn't put much energy into trying to figure it out. I got back into the car, thanked God for the little farm house with the fuel station on it and drove back to the freeway heading East. It took me twenty eight hours to drive to Cedar Rapids, Iowa form Coeur d' Alene, Idaho. From 10:00 AM one day to 4:00 PM the following day.

I encountered no other miracle, nor any difficulty. I just drove, stopped when the car needed to be fed and I fed myself as well. I didn't sleep and I didn't seam to need any rest. I arrived in great shape. After having traveled for the twenty eight hours, I still didn't get to sleep until around 3:00AM the next morning. Then, only four hours of deep sleep later, I was already preparing a slow cooking BBQ for lunch with John's employees. I seemed to just have all the energy I needed, pouring into my body.

During my five day stay, John worked his usual hours and I searched for clues to justify *going East*. I looked, listened and searched but found nothing, other than a beautiful, park-like city filled with lots of flowers, manicured lawns and kind people. I traveled around the city and beyond the city limits to open fields. I found no other magic, but the kind simplicity of Midwestern people extending warm, friendly hospitality to a stranger, as I asked for directions whenever I got lost and was ready to return to John's home at the end of the day. I was looking for something, anything to assure me that this was the place which I would soon call: home. All I felt for certain was that the rest of my life is going to be spent with John: East, West, South or North. It didn't really make any difference to me.

The five days were filled with surprises, the kind I did not even imagine and will not put to record here. I rested very little during my visit, choosing to stay as alert and observant as I could. Some of those surprises had not been positive.

John and I learned much about each other through our telephone relationship, one of which was honesty. It is remarkably easy to be honest with people while talking on the phone. For one thing, its safe . You can say whatever you need to and not have to deal with the other person's immediate reactions, like facial expressions or some other body language. A telephone can teach a person patience. Phone conversations take more time, on an average, than personal ones because they lack the physical contact, so we give the extra time, hoping that our message is received the same way it was intended. We hope to fill the lack of physical closeness with time. If things aren't going smooth enough, you can always just say: 'Good-bye,' and hang up.

During my visit, I learned more about John's life-style than the man himself. He lived quite a bit different form the way I lived. We would need to adjust. His friends were also much different from the friends I now enjoyed being with. We would need to adjust. His hobbies and recreations were also different than mine. We would need to adjust. Would we? Time and more phone conversations will tell. *For the first, time I was consciously counting on the voice without the body!*

On the morning of the sixth day we had to part and I had to leave. Go West. It sounded strange. Among all the questions in my mind, there was one certainty: I was positive that I will soon be returning. I was completely comfortable with that thought, even tough I didn't find that *other something* that I was looking for.

At 7:00 AM on Monday morning, I started the engine of my car and after one more good-bye, drove into the future. I felt contentment deep inside, knowing that everything is as it need to be.

The Heartland of this country is a home to beautiful rolling hills. In early October, she is a colorful display of shades of greens, gold and the rich oranges of turning leaves. She is also the home for much wind sweeping through the yellow stocks of still standing corn. Beautiful and peaceful - the land of much of our food source. Heartland. I drove, soaking up the warmth of the sun and the serenity of the landscape. I fed the car and myself when we needed it, then kept on driving. I made the decision to once again drive through the distance without stopping to rest. I've done it, I can do it again. At sunset, I noticed something strange happening outside of my car. I could have sworn that I was seeing worms on the top of the hood, on the side windows. Big, long, ugly black, squiggle worms all stuck to the car, some even onto the windshield. Yuck!!

'Well,' I said to myself, 'I suppose this is what might be called is hallucination. My training tells me that I am having a true *hallucination*, because there is no way that those squiggle things can possibly stay with me at the speed I am driving. It'd be a good idea to keep the windows rolled up, in any case.' I slowed down a little and so did the worms. I kept alert and watched them. Ugh, they were yukky!

"Oh- oh, now what?" The worms were changing into feathers. Every one of them!

"This is really a great trick! I suppose they are going to fly along with me at 68 mph?" I was talking out loud to myself inside of the car.

"This is it! I think I'm finally loosing my mind. All this driving, not enough sleep or even rest has finally caught up with my mind. Its either that or I must have some fantastic imagination. Now, this takes talent! Gosh, I'm good." I was half joking, half waiting to see what transpired next.

I didn't have to wait long before those feathers began to come together and take shape. I drove ahead, waited amused and filled with curiosity as those feathers came closer and closer to each other until they finally took on the perfect shape of a very large, black bird, with the wings spread wide enough to reach the entire width of the road, flapping just above the hood of the car, gliding ahead of me at 70 mph. on Interstate 90, heading West.

"If anyone would tell me a story like this one, I myself would take them to see a psychiatrist." I said and kept on driving. Each time an oncoming car or truck's headlights lit up the highway, the bird would rise above the hood of the car and disappear.   Once the vehicle passed the bird returned, flapping its wings, leading me home at 70 mph.

"This is really amazing. Really amazing! I'm gonna call this a miracle. God, I hope its not the old booze and drugs getting even with me! I never had anything like this happen to me at those times, when I had reasons, why now?" I stopped to refuel, the bird disappeared. I returned to the highway, the bird returned to the hood. After a while, I learned to follow that huge black bird with trust, until I was about 40 miles inside of the Idaho/Montana border and reached daybreak When the sun began to rise and the rays cast away the darkness, the bird simply vanished. I missed it. Crazy enough, I thanked that bird for guiding me home safe through the night and for keeping my mind occupied and alert. I was only thirty minutes away from home and as I pulled in front of my house at 6:00 AM, I realized, that the trip took only twenty three hours. After I related the trip to Catherine, she said:

"Gosh, Manonne, you always have the best stories to tell! How do you come up with them?"

I called John to let him know that I made it home, safe. Then, I went to bed and slept for eighteen hours straight.

Chapter 8

...from Spirit To Spirit...

I set a time schedule for short term plans. I allocated myself until the end of November to completely finish my home, in every detail. When I reached it, I had it listed for sale. I organized my prosperity into two categories: keepers and sharers. I was preparing to go East. I didn't know when just yet. I simply knew with the same certainty I knew long ago that one day I will get to come to America and live here. I felt as though my life truly just begun. Not because of my relationship with John, either. I just knew somewhere deep inside of me and I had no need to hurry or worry. I felt naturally comfortable.

I called Kathy for an appointment. A long one.

"Are things still rough?" There was disbelief in the tone of her voice.

"Actually, things are wonderful! I would like a past life regression." I told her.

"What do you want that for?"

"To be perfectly honest, I client of my asked me to provide that for him and even though I'm confident of the technique, I prefer to experience such a regression myself, first. At the same time, I have a conscious curiosity, we might be able to fill." She laughed sweetly, then added:

"Old habits are hard to brake. You still have to experience everything yourself, don't you?"

"I take my work very seriously. Its a huge responsibility to go inside of a human being's mind and start rearranging his past perceptions. I must be sure, every step of the way." Kathy listened with attention then said:

"You are quite something else. I am going to miss you once you're gone, but I am very happy to know not only that you chose to be a hypnotherapist but the kind of therapist you've become. There are a lot of people out there claiming to be things they are not, causing more damage and confusion, pain and negativity by pretending to know and care."

"Go ahead, Lady, keep tooting my horn." I didn't know what to do with her compliment.

Kathy and I had a wonderful and enlightening session. I found out about the difference between *soul mates and twin flames,* my *dharma* in this life, (how poorly I had been doing at it) and my purpose in my relationship with John.

I had not seen Kathy, since that November day in 1993. I became completely independent, well in body, mind and spirit, also very busy floating on the wave of God's river of life. I understood and accepted the destination of the path of that life and I had every desire to physically take part in that life. Mentally, spiritually and emotionally I was already on that path. Now, I just needed to put my physical body onto it.

God truly works in mysterious ways. He hides little clues in people, things, creatures for us to uncover and joyfully find, only to cover it up again for us to search and locate it in a different form and shape at different places, in different things.. I learned to trust and follow my spirit, that tiny, invisible God part, the essential driving force inside of me. I uncovered more and more of my own inner knowledge as I listened to the silent wisdom of my own spirit. I was finally learning my own lessons, the wonders of my inner wealth.

"...Ask and you shall receive..." But don't put requirements, restrictions, descriptions to your desires. God (your inner self, your spirit) knows far more clearly what it is you really need than your conscious mind ever could imagine. It can make it happen for you, it can make it for you.

John and I are twin flames, a complicatedly simple division of one but split wave of life energy functioning as two single manifest, now reunited with its own self.

I received John and I received myself. We grew closer and closer over the telephone. We learned more about each other (and our selves) that way, than we would have if we were physically together. The phone was our safety. One can afford to be crystal clearly honest over the phone. What could possibly happen? At worse you get hung up on.

Honesty was a big issue with us. Trust, another. Faith and belief. Acceptance was a real big issue. God was the biggest issue. We talked and we listened. John released his emotions, his fears, his hopes and dreams.
I listened. I told him mine. Did they fit together? They did.

How many twin flames are there, living on Earth right now who reunite themselves? How many who do not and are not going to in this lifetime? We are like a drop of water in the body of the mighty ocean, evaporating into parts only to continually search to become water again, reunite with its other evaporated parts to become a drop of water again. But where are those other parts? Perhaps in another ocean, a river, a pond or in a tear drop. Wherever they might be at, they will, in the endless, timeless realm of limitless eternity find themselves and reunite again and be complete, only to evaporate and evolve again and again. Isn't this a wonder?

John and I were married in August of 1994, a few days past a year of our meeting at 11:11 AM in his parents' garden. Thus began the process of our spiritual journey in healing, teaching, guiding, clarifying, transforming our own, individual selves. Two, within a unit of one, on all levels of human existence. We are here to perfect our human selves, our souls or egos, through the purification and upliftment of that soul into the spiritual realm of God's Kingdom on Earth. We have a bright and shining yet silent and wise spirit along with a curious, mischievous and most often disobedient soul, united to live in a complex, well constructed and durable temple we call body. As human beings, we are two volunteers of: a master spirit and student ego, teaching and learning at the same instant. The human experience is much like having a wise old seer riding in a New York City rush - hour traffic with a lively teenager at the steering wheel! Either way - seer or teenager - it surely is an experience!

Driving on the highway of life with John has taught me much, already. John has taught me much. Most importantly, John has taught me the pure meaning of unconditional love. I was familiar with the concept of the expression and I certainly used it often in my lectures, teachings and healing practice. But to feel it deep within all of the fibers of my entire being - John, without his own conscious awareness has taught me to experience such a rich feeling. I am grateful to him for that wisdom within him. John also taught me more patience than an ancient man watching a blade of grass grow, ever could have. What has he learned from me? I wouldn't even guess. That would be up to him to express, if he so chooses.

I do know that he accepted God and God's love as he saw him through my eyes. He accepted my lifestyle without questioning and he is seemingly comfortable in it. We accepted each other without the desire to change each other.

I go to open AA meetings with him and he comes to my Spiritual Healing Center. I watch him bowl and golf and he makes a treasure map with me. We walk along the river bend and we meditate together. I travel and lecture and give service and he is in the audience because he desires to be there. I travel across the country with him and he travels across the universe with me.

We listen to each other's day's events and we listen to the subliminal tapes with the waterfalls.

As we grow spiritually, we find ourselves filled with more and more energy of happiness and joy and freedom coming from the one and only source: God. We come to

God with trust and faith, belief and openness rather than fear and desperation. New life and new love flows through us each moment of our timeless time. It keeps us lively, funny, happy and healthy, looking and feeling younger every day. It keeps us creative and fills us with expectancy, instead of expectations. Every breath is our divine spiritual practice. Every step brings us closer to a real fulfillment packed with courage, discipline and purpose to easily conquer the obstacles laying across our own paths of life.

Each of us are wonderful teachers and students to both our selves and one another. Our circumstances are our classrooms . Do you like the classroom you are in now? If not, change it. I did. We must always remember that God gives all of us millions of choices to select from. We are never ever stuck in one classroom. If you are not learning to your highest benefit, change your classroom until you walk through the door of you own inner wisdom. Choose another classroom.   There are many different ways to learn the same lessons. Change your circumstances if you need to. Be a strong, deciplined teacher to yourself. Be the master, not the servant.

Do not settle. Accept and be peaceful or make that change for your highest good You have the power and the tools inside of yourself to manifest all of your desires, to learn all of your lessons.

We have manifested much in the past three and a half years. One moment after another. We manifested each other into a sober, clean, healthy and happy life within a new life style that is comfortable for both of us. Emotional tranquillity. We learned to balance our egos and our spirits. We created individual independence within our unit of two. We manifested a new home with a huge back yard where John tends to keep the lawn the greenest possible and I grow beautiful flowers to soothe the soul and share with friends and clients. In the summer we sit among the flower beds as I teach meditation classes and we listen to the songs of birds and the humming of the bees. We have manifested the love and trust of our families and new friends. But most of all, we manifested truth and reality as we had not known existed before.

I had manifested my healing center and I am very busy in it. Most of my clients are substance abusers and other dysfunctional souls still in very much emotional pain. I hypnotize them, reverse the perception of the ego's input and with time and some more therapy and reinforcement they no longer say that they are alcoholics, substance abusers or dysfunctional. (I consider food, cigarettes, medications, relationships, negative attitudes, in fact anything in access which an individual habitually depends on as substance.)

With hypnotherapy and positive subliminal messages I had changed my life. I do not miss the drugs, alcohol, cigarettes, food or destructive relationships I once craved for, worshipped and convinced myself that I could not live without. I know that I now could not live with those evils in my life, ever again.

Today, new scientific evidence proves to us that 98% of our body cells are naturally replaced in less than one year! The cells which I once soaked in alcohol and drugs (prescribed or not), fumigated with four packs of cigarette smoke per day, filled with junk food are long, long dead and gone. So, how could I have been so deeply addicted?

You are not addicted to the substance, you are addicted to the memory of the experience

What does this mean? As I understand it and believe it, the drug, alcohol or any substance for that matter is the antidote to the chemical manifested in the body (manufactured, if you will). The memory of the experience is not the substance itself but the recollection of the altered

246

state of conscious or emotional identification. What we remember is, that when the substance enters the body the emotion begins to change, it becomes duller, more removed from reality and the pain. But how does the pain get there in the first place?

My explanation is going to be very basic and childish, not for your benefit, simply because this is the only way I know how to relate it through my own personal experiences.

At the beginning of this book I laid down the truth of my life. On the conscious level, I thought and believed that I was living a naturally comfortable (normal) life. On the subconscious level, the level of spiritual knowledge I knew it was not true. Therefore, from the spirit came a nudge to the ego: 'things aren't honest around here, you better do something about it!' Not having long enough living experiences at that time yet, my ego didn't know what was wrong. On the surface things seemed fine, because they were accepted by all others around me. The ego was content at receiving whatever it received, having no ability do evaluate, judge and determine the truth of my circumstance. So, it let it be. But the spirit kept signaling, the ego kept ignoring and there was the making of the inner war. The spirit trying to do its job of teaching, the ego not having exposure to natural function, refusing to pay attention to the teacher. Each time the ego ignored the spirit sent a jolt of self manufactured chemical through the body as a reminder. That inner chemical then caused a physical or emotional sensation which was not naturally comfortable. After a while, having learned that my spirit's yearning for my mother's love will be dulled soon after I drank the wine, I not only accepted the wine, but yearned to use it to fend off all other discomforts and pain. I taught myself through proven experiences that the presence of alcohol represented the absence of pain.

I became addicted not to the presence of alcohol, but to the absence of pain.

I didn't gradually learn how to deal with natural human development, instead I learned how to avoid it.

I addicted myself to the lack of natural development. The more my ego denied, the more my spirit corrected, the more evident the war became, the more my ego had to use to succeed at the denial process. My ego was busy. My spirit had a full time job fixing, correcting, finding new ways, new internal chemicals, inventing new dis - eases to remind my ego to get on with her job of learning . In tern my ego had to keep looking for new ways to shut down the system and make the pain go away. I was busy. Both parts of me working overtime just to get by, never mind get ahead.

Addiction to any substance is rooted in the ego's inability the admit that it had been perceived the external life incorrectly, feeding incorrect information into the memory bank. Simply put, not learning the lessons well. Not unlike a kid in school. By not doing the homework correctly in the first place, the teacher will insist that the student goes back to study and do it right and will keep insisting until it is done right. If the student learns, the test is passed and things move on smooth. If the student ignores the lesson, he will fall farther and farther behind until he becomes overwhelmed, over burdened, stressed, scared and helpless. He will not know how to go on because he didn't learn how to survive gradually, he didn't learn to be an independent human being. All he learned was how to cover up own mistakes, his own inaccurate perceptions. He learned to dodge his responsibilities.

I have affectionately named this lack in perceptual input: E.D.D.S. or Emotional Development Deficiency Syndrome.

No person is required to experience the extent of the pain and traumas that I had experienced to develop E.D.D.S. An un-nurtured child, a miss-informed child, a miss-treated child is very likely to develop some 'ism' or E.D.D.S. and train itself to grow dysfunctional. The importance lay not in the actual experience, but in the perception, in the interpretation of the experience. What will register in the subconscious memory bank is how the ego perceives the external, before it sends that interpretation into the storage chambers of the subconscious for processing. If there is a 'miss' information, it will be returned for correction. My job is to find the incorrect input, reverse the unnatural or negatively perceived memory, replace it with target truth more in line with the acceptance of the subconscious mind and turn off the manufacturing of the internal chemical. My job is to make ease from dis - ease. It is that simple - if we are willing.

A few years ago I was treating a young man in his early twenties. It appeared that each year, near the time of his birthday he would become very lonely, withdrawn, irritable and depressed. He'd be angry and overly critical of himself. He told me that he felt a deep sense of pain, but this pain was really in no particular distinguishable place in his physical body. It just hung onto him someplace inside. He couldn't show me, he could only tell me. Even that, he couldn't do very well. Though he was not a regular drinker, he did get and stayed drunk for weeks during these times. He had been doing this since he was about twelve years old. He would start thinking of his natural mother (without consciously thinking, he told me that he was adopted as a child) and there would surface that pain and without a thought he would follow his feet to the nearest bar and get drunk. He wouldn't just have a few drinks, he would get down right sloppy drunk. For the rest of the year he would not drink any alcohol at all, he tried convincing me but around the time of his birthday, his emotional world simply fell apart. I believed him.

All this information he volunteered to share with me, during his first visit, which started out somewhat stressed. He had already been pretty busy with his drinking that day and the devilish alcohol played its game of hide and seek, altering his personality from belligerence to cooperation, changing from moment to moment. I understood it and we played the game for about an hour. He then began to sober a little and I was able to get a conscious commitment for him as he realized the reason he was in my office in the first place.

Hypnotizing him in that condition was out of all considerations, so I needed a commitment from him to return to my office the following day. Since I was able to create a level of trust in him, he agreed. I proceeded to relax him through his own breathing and gave him instructions how to practice the same breathing at home and until he saw me again, the next day. He understood that he had to be sober for any hypnotic induction, otherwise I would not work with him. He seemed to understand that as well. He relaxed enough to enjoy the feeling and it gave him enough memory to look forward to the following day. He had to return in a sober state and on time for the appointment.

He did do just that! Sober and on time! Good job. We established trust and respect already, two essential components for effective and long lasting therapy.

While in the regressed state, he revealed his first memories of what I believed had been the hidden cause of his recurring, seemingly unbearable pain. He brought himself back to the time and select experience of his body being handed over to his adopting mother . He was only two days old. I locked onto his words as I kept asking him specific questions and I clearly understood that his subconscious mind vividly recorded the event as abandonment and rejection. Given away, being an unwanted baby, a mistake to get rid of! Though I was not adopted, I understood the depth of that pain very well.

My responsibility was to reverse that perception and to create a final and permanent understanding of the same experience without lying to his subconscious, which would cause more pain and confusion for him in the future. I had to reverse his memory from being given away to being received, from being a toss - away to being a gift. I had to convince both his conscious and subconscious mind that he was created to be a precious gift of life which his natural mother provided to his adopting parents.

By the end of the session, he visually wrapped himself in a gift box, wrapped in Christmas paper. (His birthday was on December 26th.) I suggested to him that form that moment on he will see himself as a much wanted gift and he will love himself for being such a gift.

He left with two appropriate waterfall tapes to replace my words and strengthen his self esteem. One year later, undisturbed by his birthday, he was sober as he called and asked if I would unite him and his fiancee in marriage He accepted the truth as it really was and he accepted himself for the young man he really was.

Not every one of my stories are as cute as this one is. Some are pretty colorful and some are down right ugly. But every story has two sides, this I know from personal experience - depending on the perception.

I remember very clearly, the last time I had an alcoholic beverage. It was on January 14, 1994. I am not remembering that I got drunk, I am remembering when I drank it. I had a glass of wine at a Christmas party. It was not a very good wine (believe me, I know what I'm talking about) but I drank it anyway. As the waiter came around to collect the empty glasses I placed mine on the tray and nodded my head in agreement for another glass of wine, without stopping to think. When he returned with the full glass and set it down in front of me I was genuinely surprised!

'Why did I do this?' I asked myself. 'I didn't even enjoy the first one!'

I sat there in the room filled with close to one hundred people, in amazement. As I looked around I found the answer. Everyone else in that room was drinking alcohol. It was 'the thing to do'. Directly in front of me stood 'the memory of the experience' in physical form, even though I had no pain to dull. Doing the things that other people do, just because. Because we don't know how to be our selves and relax with that awareness, because we want to be like others, we want to be part of their thing, we want to fit in and be accepted. I had no physical or emotional negativity, I simply fell into the motion and rhythm of other people. No, thank you! I stood up from the table and poured the wine into a pot of a nearby fig tree, walked up to the bar and ordered a glass of cranberry juice which I thoroughly enjoyed. I did not ask anyone else to follow suit.

I had achieved peace, understanding and acceptance of myself and others around me. Now, my ego is completely relaxed about alcohol, drugs, food, cigarettes and everything else I know is not for my benefit.

I still listen to the waterfall tapes every day, but today the messages are more in the areas of prosperity, loving and feeling loved and laughter. I figure, one can never have too much love and joy, right?

I am not a phonetic about anything I'm aware of and my only addiction is to God and God alone. You are welcome to call me a junky, because this addiction I am not willing to surrender to any human or immortal being. To this addiction I am committed!

When I have a desire, I am able to declare my intention, make a commitment to it, put my attention on it and patiently wait to gracefully accept the outcome. This is how I practice what I learned formally and experientially. Everything is possible if we allow ourselves to believe that it is possible even if that something is quite out of the ordinary.

I found what I believed I needed. I needed someone like Kathy, I needed tapes to whisper to me things which I still am not aware of, consciously. I needed God in my conscious awareness. I couldn't do it alone, struggling on the bumpy road of my life, worn out by my own false efforts. I needed to make the change for me and through that change I was able to offer my true self, my love, my kindness and nurturing to all those who asked me for it.

Believe and God will reward you in direct proportion to your belief.

If you need God or your own Kathy, reach out for them. They are there. If you have to search, then search but please, don't give up! You too, deserve to be as happy and free as I am.

Search, seek, ask questions and don't worry about doubting until you find what and who feels naturally comfortable to you to accept temporary guidance from.

We do not need to think that we must be lucky or fortunate or unfortunate people to have or not have all that we desire. God truly has created us all equally with the same breath of life and river of knowledge. We are all born with it. We can all find it inside, not outside. It comes from the depth of our immortal essence, rather than from the acceptance and approval of another human being. We all have the same unlimited, immeasurable power to make changes in accordance with our beliefs. This power is with us day and night, awake and asleep. It is ready to be put into action to benefit our selves as well as all created kind.

Beloved child of God, allow yourself the possibility of a greater, happier, more fulfilled you, even if you think you are as great now as you can ever be. Love yourself with your own wisdom and through that love you also love God, for God is ever present, forever part of you. And with that love I know that you love me and everyone and everything else in creation as I love you, for we are all made of the essential sameness in spirit, connected and inseparable.

It is our ego or soul, which keeps us individuals and apart. It is that unique, foreign substance in us that makes the judgment and prejudice.

Could we look deeper into our similarities, rather than judge the differences?   I look forward to that consciousness. Patiently, I look forward to it.

Today, the voice without the body is saying to me:
"The Kingdom of God is in your essence, not in the ethers. Heaven on Earth is living in balance between your Spirit and your Ego, between your God self and your Soul self right here, right now. Look not to the sky for your Heaven, rather look inside your consciousness. Where ever you are, there is your Heaven or Hell on Earth, depending on your state of consciousness.   When you are within your Spiritual consciousness, you are in Heaven. Then, where ever you are, love is, where ever you are God is.

With God, everything is.
I Love You, One and All.

Chapter 9

One Last Test

Kelly is now married and she is a mother of two little boys: Jason and Lexi. Our relationship had been an ongoing up and down for most of our lives.

During the summer of 1995, John and I decided to visit Kelly and her little family. We were all pretty exited about the trip. We flew into Spokane, WA, rented a car and drove the 40 miles to see my kids! Already late in the evening, we checked into a motel and I called Kelly from the room to let them know that we arrived safely. We were going to her home for breakfast the next morning.

I was still asleep when the phone rang with its typical loud, alarming sound and startled me out of my wonderful dream.

"Hello." I answered it sleepily.

"Hello, Mom? Are you awake?" Kelly asked.

" Hi, Honey, its morning already?" I tried to wake up.

"Guess who I have been talking to all morning?" Too early for questions, I thought.

"Why don't you just tell me, Honey." I sat up in bed to encourage my coming alive.

"My father. I have been talking with my father."

"Which one?" I had been married so many times, she had a collection of fathers.

"The real one. I have been talking with my real father, Michael."

"Kelly, Honey, don't do…"

"Mom, remember a few months ago, I asked you for some information about my grandfather, in New York? Well, I wrote to the place you said he used to work at and I got an answer. He had retired many years ago, but the man who makes out his pension checks wrote back to me and said that he now lives in Florida and if I write a letter directly to my grandfather, he will include the it with the next check, so I did. Today I got a call not from my grandfather but my father! Isn't it great? He said that he's been looking for me in the past few months. Kelly was exited, thrilled and everything else you could imagine she could be.

All I could think of was: 'where has he been for the last twenty seven years? I believed that he died long ago. I didn't know that he was alive but he new that we were. I had no reason to look for him, he could have looked for us. All Kelly ever wanted was a daddy - why didn't he find her before, why look for her now? Where was he when a little girl needed him? All through those years when she was saving her allowance, and one day she came to me and handed me her little savings and asked me to go and by her a nice Daddy. He knew that he was alive, why didn't he look for her then! How come he couldn't find her when she was still a little girl in need! How very easy it is now to walk into her life as a full grown woman!' I know that I should have been happy for Kelly but I couldn't. She sensed my emotions in my voice, my pauses, even through my breathing.

"You are the most selfish woman I have ever known, " she said. "I suggest that you stay away from me, my children, my family for a while. I think its best that you don't contact us, just forget about us!" She was filled with anger, resentment and a lot more hate for me than I ever felt from her before.

"I would still like to bring over the children's presents, though." I was just as hurt as she, for different reasons which she could not have understood. After Kelly hung up the phone, I kept sitting on the bed, wondering what actually happened? My world fell apart in less than five minutes.

Twenty seven years ago, someone lied to me about the father of my child. I believed him. For twenty seven years I wondered what could life had been if my child knew her father. Would we had a life together? Would we have become a family? Would we had more children? Suddenly none of that mattered. Life was what it was, is what it is and will be what it will be. He had his reasons to stay away all through these years as well as he had his reasons for returning to her life at this time. Everything in this world happens for a specific purpose, known or unknown to us.

I was beginning to feel a sense of joy for Kelly, though I didn't tell her. Eventually, all things unfold without my doing anything about them. I realized that Michael had nothing to do with my life right now. He was a stranger, returning from the past and he returned not to me but to Kelly. My life was going to go on precisely as it was scheduled to go on before this new development. I was not interested in what Michael looked like, what his thoughts were, what he did or not do. I felt suddenly comfortable with everything about the situation and myself. I felt peaceful.

Nearly a year later, when Kelly finally made her decision to call me, she sounded totally different. She told me then, that she missed talking with me and without any big expectations of apologies or forgiveness, she returned to my life, family and all. Today, we have a mature, loving relationship, where each of us are open and willing to hear the other's point of view without aggression. I often ask for her point of view and she asks for mine. She finally has her mother and her father, even though her parents no longer know each other.

Once, when she was about seventeen years old, she said to me in a heat of anger:

"There is nothing about you that I can respect. At the time, I was hurt and angry with her. Today, we respect each other, like each other and love each other, even though often we do not understand each other. That is more, than I can ask from anyone. Being accepted and loved for precisely who I am is the greatest honor and gift. When I feel these attitudes radiating from several different directions, I am sustain in my mind that there is such a thing as unconditional love and forgiveness. But most of all, deep in my heart I know that even if things were not this way, it still wouldn't matter, because God is within me and everything always is as it should be. Sooner or later we will all recognize the power of this, most precious moment we are now living in.. This very moment is all we ever really have.. Loving this moment and everything in it is my gift of eternal life and the joy of my presence.

Afterwards

I wrote this book as simply and honestly as I could. I used words to keep the contents easily understandable, hopefully lifting some of the stress its message may cause.

The purpose of writing this book was to let the reader know that life never is the same from two different view points, even when the same eyes are looking at that life. If the reader has a need similar to that of this writer, than let's not look and compare the details of the assumed experiences, but look at the opportunities to fulfill that need, whatever its origin. I urge the reader to question any new direction he or she might take. Question even this writer and be certain that the words, the messages feel naturally comfortable. Ask for references and credentials, ask for an interview, go to a public speaking of your potential new guide or therapist before you surrender your mind to her or him. Do not allow yourself to be more confused than perhaps you already are. Simplify things in you life with letting go, not complicate by taking on more confusion and endless stress..

Hypnotism is a powerful tool in healing when it is applied properly and with professional expertise. The clearing of one's mind of the negative clutter is one of the most wonderful and healing experiences this writer has subjected her own self to and received unimagined results. Hypnotherapy has no negative side effects, it is safe and it can be permanent, providing the subject with freedom from all forms of dependencies. Hypnotherapy can be utilized to ease stress and depression, physical pain and discomfort and in some cases even control terminal illnesses, just to mention a few applications. There is very little scientific data that is available, yet. We are gathering data every day, all over the world. Until science invents the appropriate equipment to measure the application and results of such wonderful therapy, I urge the reader to research the service provider to the reader's total satisfaction.

Only a few year ago chiropractic had not been accepted as a healing alternative to medicine. Today, it is.

Not long before that, psychology was also frowned upon and those who ventured to consult one were often labeled as nuts or crazy. Today, more and more people seek out the services of a Ph. D.

I eagerly look forward to the time - in the very near future - when hypnotherapists are also recognized as trained, knowledgeable and respected professionals of the healing field in human services.

With Love, Light and Perfect Health,

The Reverend L. Manonne Fontainne, O. M., C. Ht.

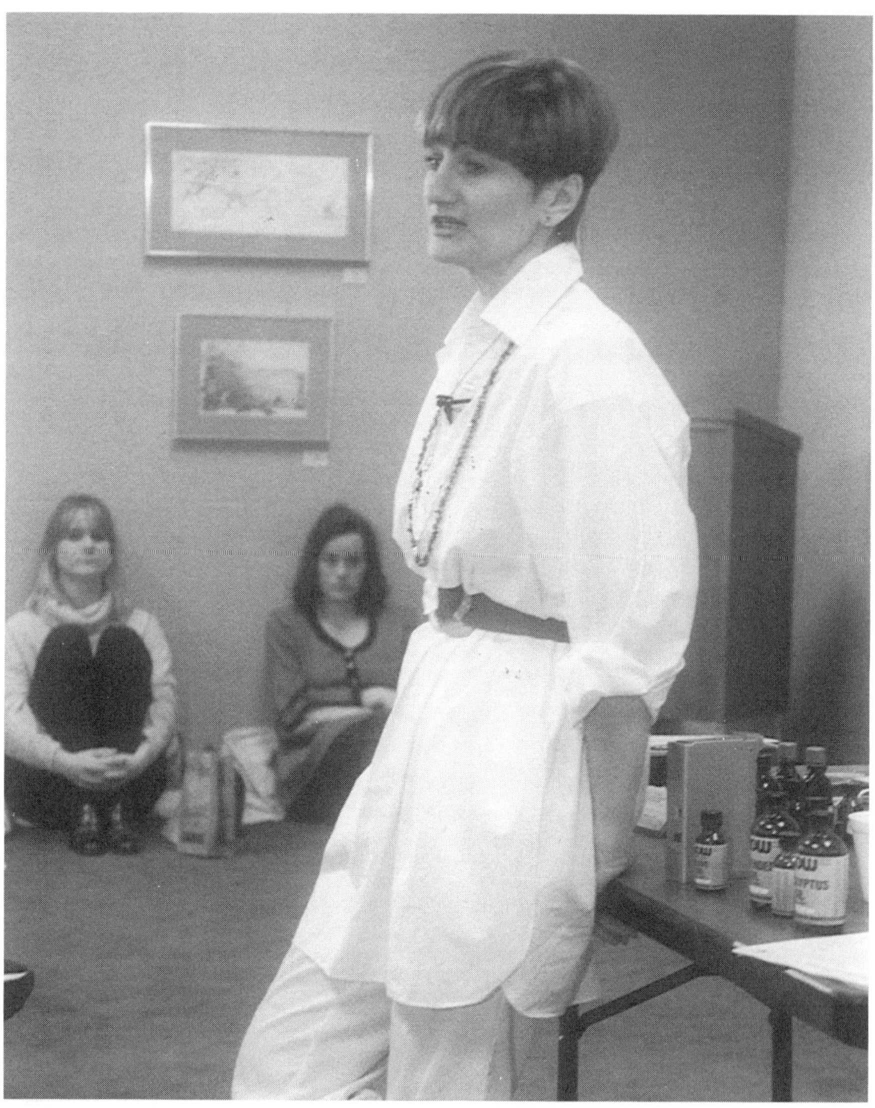

When there are no empty seats left, listeners stay and choose to sit on the floor. I love them all. Cedar Rapids Public Library.

Questions and answers. Young or old, there is time to learn, to expend, to decide to change our mind...